THE
SCHOOL
OF THE
CHURCH

THE
SCHOOL
OF THE
CHURCH

Worship and
Christian Formation

PHILIP H. PFATTEICHER

TRINITY PRESS INTERNATIONAL
Valley Forge, Pennsylvania

for
Thomas Joseph McDermott IV
and
Ian Robert Pfatteicher Conlin
whose mothers will find themselves
in these pages

Copyright © 1995 Philip H. Pfatteicher

Trinity Press International, P. O. Box 851, Valley Forge, PA 19482–0851

Library of Congress Cataloging-in-Publication Data
Pfatteicher, Philip H.
    The school of the Church : worship and Christian formation /
Philip H. Pfatteicher.
        p.   cm.
    Includes bibliographical references and index.
    ISBN 1-56338-110-9 (pbk.)
    1. Liturgics. 2. Language and languages—Religious aspects—
Christianity. 3. Music—Religious aspects—Christianity.
4. Worship (Religious education). 5. Christian education.
6. Lutheran Church—Liturgy. I. Title.
BV178.P45   1995
264'.001—dc20   94-47514
                                                          CIP

Printed in the United States of America

95   96   97   98   99   10   9   8   7   6   5   4   3   2   1

CONTENTS

~ ✛ ~

PREFACE

~ ✠ ~

THIS BOOK may be understood as a meditation upon a statement by Gregory Dix:

> It is only by entering into that universal christian mind and thinking with it that we modern christians enter into the fullness of our christian inheritance.[1]

Such an entrance requires a certain humility, a modest view of one's own achievements and abilities, a willingness to submit to a course of instruction, training, and formation under the guidance of our spiritual ancestors from a vast variety of times and places and cultures. It requires a receptive attitude together with a lifetime of studious prayer and prayerful study. The Christian liturgy most of all provides a powerful, deeply evocative expression of "the fullness of our Christian inheritance." It is there that one learns most suggestively what Christianity is all about.

The nineteenth-century German scholar Hermann Jacoby understood Luther's view of worship to be "an institute of the mature in faith for the training of the immature."[2] Such a division was an unfortunate German tradition, reflected in Leipzig in Bach's time where there was a separation between the "mature" (*geföderte*) Christians who needed no private confession and the "immature" Christians who did.[3] That curious definition may be acceptable only if one understands that we are all among the "immature." Insofar as Jacoby's definition separates the church into two groups, the grown-ups, satisfied with their maturity, and the growing who have a way to go, it is destructive of authentic Christianity. To say, as will be argued in the following pages, that the liturgy is a school is emphatically not to say that the model is the classroom with the minister as teacher and the congregation as a class. Still less is it true that the minister is a performer and the congregation an audience, the entertainer and the entertained. Such a gulf between minister and people is at least no longer acceptable. The whole congregation, minister and people, in their interaction are confronted by large and ancient discoveries and truths, and it is in that multifaceted confrontation that the church, clergy and laity together, the whole people of God, learns and grows.

"Liturgy" as it is used in this book is to be understood not simply as any service of worship or any service that follows a recognizable and predictable order. "Liturgy," as it is used here, is a regularly repeated and predictable order of worship, a defining characteristic of a denomination or confession, a clearly identifiable and recognizable continuation of the historic form of Eucharist and Office (Daily Prayer) of the catholic church of the West and of the East. This historic form itself derives in large measure from the worship of the synagogue (*synaxis*) and the family prayer of early Judaism (the Great Thanksgiving). Moreover, the richness of the liturgy includes not only the general shape and pattern of such rites but also movement and gesture, music and silence, and, indeed, particular texts, some well known, such as the Lord's Prayer, the Nicene Creed, and the Sanctus, and others less familiar, such as individual Verses, Offertories, and Responsories. To many outside the liturgical tradition this may seem a narrow and confining understanding, but as the following pages I hope will show, it is in fact a wonderfully enriching and liberating tradition. In fact, it is such grounding, rootedness, and continuity that makes growth possible. "Thank God I'm not free," exclaimed D. H. Lawrence, "any more than a rooted tree is free."[4]

There is abroad an unhappiness with liturgical forms, especially in a number of the "liturgical" churches, born of a lack of appreciation of what the liturgy is and does, as well as a lack of understanding of what the church is, indeed, of what Christianity is. To make the church's worship seem inviting to modern people many have taken to revising or rewriting the liturgy on an individual or congregational basis to make the language more acceptable to contemporary sensitivities and concerns. Before such alteration takes place, however, if it is to be a clear improvement, widespread study, discussion, and reflection must take place across denominational and confessional lines, for the liturgy is the property of the whole church. Changing language is generally not the place to begin. It is too easy, and it is too deceptive.

The liturgy as it is understood in these pages is, frankly, an acquired taste, and it is none the worse for that. This book, therefore, is a prolegomenon to the study of liturgy. It is intended to provide a basic understanding of what the liturgy is and does and to lay the groundwork for more detailed historical, theological, and linguistic examinations of the worship of the Christian church.

•

When I was writing my *Commentary on the Lutheran Book of Worship: Lutheran Liturgy in Its Ecumenical Context* (Minneapolis: Augsburg Fortress, 1990), Frank Senn suggested that I include a chapter on language. That book grew too large for the inclusion of such a chapter, but the present volume is a development of what such a chapter might have said. In this, as in so much else, I continue to be in Dr. Senn's debt. I am moreover grateful to several groups at whose invitation I had opportunity to reflect upon many of the issues addressed in this book. Among them have been the Third Annual *Ad Fontes* Conference, April 30, 1988, in Ephrata, Pennsylvania; the Region I Conference of the Association of Lutheran Church Musicians hosted by Muhlenberg College and St. John's Church, Allentown, Pennsylvania, July 6–8, 1988; the 1989 Institute of Liturgical Studies at Valparaiso University, at which I gave the keynote address honoring Herbert Lindemann; the 1989 Annual Theological Consultation of the Southwestern Pennsylvania Synod of the Evangelical Lutheran Church in America. I owe particular gratitude to Bishop Donald J. McCoid, who suggested that I address the consultation as theologian in residence, for his gracious hospitality while I was resident on the territory of his synod.

In this book, which makes connections between literature and liturgy, it is appropriate for me to record my gratitude to my friend and teacher, Benjamin H. DeMott, who, it is little exaggeration to say, taught me how to read, and to another friend, Donald Hall, whose exemplary text *Writing Well,* has since its first edition been my constant companion in the composition classroom. Each in his own way also takes religion seriously.

I am grateful moreover to the students in my classes in myth and ritual; in literature, especially poetry; the literature of Greece and Rome, the Orient, the Native Americans. Through a quarter-century they have put up with my probing of texts, relationships, and meaning in pursuit of my conviction, with Carlyle, that "Literature is but a branch of Religion."

Chapter One

THE LANGUAGE
OF THE LITURGY

H OLY ASSEMBLIES must not use any foreign language, the Second
Helvetic Confession (1562) declared; all things should be put
forth in a language understood by the congregation.[1] The declaration
seems unexceptionable. It has been a principal tenet of the churches
of the Reformation that the people must understand the language of
worship. The Roman Catholic Church since the Second Vatican Council shares this concern, and, increasingly, in the Orthodox churches also
old languages give way to the language the congregation actually speaks
in ordinary life. The people must understand the liturgy if it is indeed
to be their work.

Translation is therefore a continuing necessity. Liturgical expression
must be moved from one language to another, from one culture to another, from one age to another. This continuous necessity of translation
is, however, an exceedingly complex task. In some ways no wholly satisfying translation is ever possible. (Robert Frost was fond of defining
poetry as "that which is lost in translation."[2]) Perhaps the best one can
hope for is an adequate approximation.

Learning a New Language

The requirement of continuous translation lays several problems on the
whole church. Because translation by its very nature can never be entirely satisfactory and since it is impractical to require converts to learn
the ancient language (and what would it be — Latin, Greek, Aramaic?),
we can neither simply revert to the past nor expect everything to be
made plain for us in our familiar tongue. We must learn a new language
that is natural to very few in the modern world.

1

In the process of continual translation and interpretation, one set of problems has to do with the translation of ancient texts. Usually for the Western church this means the translation of Latin into English. Some have lamented this necessity. Luther Reed reports the remark of Edward T. Horn concerning the Gregorian collect formerly assigned in the Roman, Anglican, and Lutheran rites to the First Sunday after the Epiphany: "Such a collect makes one wish that we always said our prayers in Latin."[3] Finding English equivalents for Latin words and phrases is only the beginning. More perplexing is finding language that is satisfying in English for itself and not only because it renders the Latin in an acceptable way. The *Book of Common Prayer* of 1549 established a style that the present American *Book of Common Prayer* (1979) continues, although in two forms, traditional and contemporary, betraying a certain uneasiness with changing what it had established as the classic style of prayer in English. An example is the translation of a collect from the Gregorian sacramentary (no. 922).[4] The 1979 Prayer Book assigns the collect to the Fourth Sunday after the Epiphany and gives it both in "traditional" translation,

> Almighty and everlasting God, who dost govern all things in heaven and earth: Mercifully hear the supplications of thy people, and in our time grant us thy peace; through Jesus Christ our Lord, who liveth and reigneth with thee and the Holy Spirit, one God, for ever and ever. (164)

and in "contemporary" form,

> Almighty and everlasting God, you govern all things both in heaven and earth: Mercifully hear the supplications of your people, and in our time grant us your peace; through Jesus Christ our Lord, who lives and reigns with you and the Holy Spirit, one God, for ever and ever. (215)

The *Lutheran Book of Worship* (1978) appoints the prayer for the Eighth Sunday after the Epiphany; it has moved somewhat further along the line of adapting the traditional English rendering of the prayer and employs a straightforward, even blunt style:

> Almighty and everlasting God, ruler of heaven and earth: Hear our prayer and give us your peace now and forever; through your Son, Jesus Christ our Lord.

The Roman Catholic Church, through its International Commission on English in the Liturgy (ICEL), began the task of translating the revised mass and propers into English without relying on the translations into English of other liturgical churches. It is now at work revising the translations of 1973 in a more conservative and more sensitive way, moving notably closer to the language of the Anglican and Lutheran service books. The Roman rite now appoints the collect as the opening prayer for the Second Sunday in Ordinary Time. The earlier translation was

> Father of heaven and earth,
> hear our prayers,
> and show us the way to peace in the world.
> Grant this through our Lord Jesus Christ,
>   your Son,
> who lives and reigns with you
>   and the Holy Spirit,
> one God, for ever and ever.

The revision of April 1, 1988 is

> Almighty God,
> whose never-failing providence rules all things
> both in heaven and on earth,
> listen to the cry of your people
> and govern in peace the course of our days.
>
> Grant this through our Lord Jesus Christ,
>   your Son,
> who lives and reigns with you in the unity
>   of the Holy Spirit,
> God for ever and ever.[5]

The commission originally thought that the achievement of a satisfactory liturgical translation would take time to achieve. The revisions indicate that they have found the path and that it leads through the existing translations of other churches.

A second set of problems in translation involves moving from older forms of English to a more contemporary mode. Even the matter of replacing Tudor verb forms with modern forms is not as straightforward as it may at first seem. *Agnus Dei, qui tollis peccata mundi,* "Lamb of God, who taketh away the sin of the world," is not to be rendered,

"Lamb of God, who takes away the sin of the world," for "taketh" is second person, and in modern dress the clause would be "Lamb of God, who take away the sin of the world." But this is a form never in use, and it sounds ungrammatical to the modern ear, suggesting an illiterate question rather than a statement. The revision in the *Lutheran Book of Worship* of William H. Draper's translation of Francis of Assisi's hymn "All Creatures of Our God and King" makes that mistake in stanza 4 in translating "unfoldeth" of the original translation: "Dear mother earth, who day by day / Unfolds rich blessings on our way..." To be grammatically if not aesthetically correct the word should be "unfold." The translation of such relative clauses, common in the antecedent reason (basis for petition) of the collect form, is, therefore, in moving toward contemporary speech, usually changed to a direct second-person address, "Lamb of God, you take away the sin of the world." This is a form we use in paying compliments ("You do that very well"; "You have been a great comfort to me") and when we rebuke someone ("You should never have done that!"; "You have been a naughty child!") The old verb forms are troublesome nowadays, and errors slip past even careful proofreaders. It is not unusual that a free prayer offered in the present day but in the old language will exhibit grammatical errors.

A third set of problems, even more basic than the complex matters of moving from ancient to modern language and from old to contemporary grammar, has to do with learning a new and largely foreign language, the language of symbolism. Eric Fromm recognized the problem that has eviscerated ritual and many traditional stories as well and responded to it in his book *The Forgotten Language: An Introduction to the Understanding of Dreams, Fairy Tales, and Myths* (1951). The forgotten language of which he writes is the language of symbols, "the only universal language the human race ever developed."[6] It is this task of learning again the forgotten language of ritual and symbol that the present book addresses. Beneath the matters — as important as they are — of inclusive language and the naming of God is a still more fundamental and necessary requirement. We must learn again what it means to have a liturgy, to use receptively forms inherited from our predecessors in the faith, to give ourselves to somewhat alien patterns of doing and thinking in order to stretch our spirits and ignite our imagination.

A principal glory of the Lutheran Common Service of 1888 was its wholeness. Lutherans coming to North America, having no English tradition of their own to draw on, had to learn to use English in worship.

In the Common Service and its predecessor English rites, biblical readings (Epistle and Gospel) and biblical texts (Introit and Gradual) were
from what was then the standard English translation of the Bible, the
Authorized (King James) Version of 1611, and the style and language
of the other parts of the liturgy (collects, addresses and exhortations,
prayers) were influenced by and echoed the stately rhythms of that
"noblest monument of English prose."[7] This version had set the standard for liturgical English for centuries. The culmination of a century
of English translations of the Bible, it was

> a prose of considerable range, drawing as occasion demands on
> both sides of the renaissance conception of the use of English, the
> native continuity and humanist virtuosity. Structurally, it leans
> toward Alfredian simplicity. In vocabulary it tends to be archaic,
> verging on archaic even as Tyndale wrote it and certainly archaic
> when his language was reprinted in 1611. From the beginning it
> was a special kind of prose. For all its structural simplicity, and
> however concrete and homely its illustrations, it was never the
> language of everyday life. The sacredness of the subject-matter
> and the setting in which it was heard kept it apart.[8]

The translators of the Lutheran liturgy in 1888 were conscious of their
responsibility and privilege to participate in the maintenance of a grand
tradition of translation, crowned, some would say completed,[9] in 1611
by King James's committee.

But already in the seventeenth century writers were aware of and
distressed by the rapid change of the language. Edmund Waller in 1688
could write "Of English Verse,"

> But who can hope his lines should long
> Last in a daily changing tongue?
>
> Poets that lasting marble seek
> Must carve in Latin or in Greek;
> We write in sand, our language grows,
> And like the tide our work o'erflows.

As the centuries passed and the King James language receded farther
into the past and became not only archaic but obscure and in places
even misleading, the desire was expressed for a new translation. The
result has been, of course, a flood of translations in the twentieth century; the changes in Bible translation naturally spilled over into the

liturgy in which the Bible was read and helped to encourage change
in that language as well. By the middle of the twentieth century, the
preeminent Lutheran liturgist Luther Reed was aware that it was going
to be difficult to preserve the old Authorized Version and its language,
and he warned of the impending crisis.

> Among the larger general questions that will probably arise will be
> the matter of Scripture versions. Those whose approach to corpo-
> rate worship is literal and pedagogical rather than devotional and
> liturgical will be ready to make a hodge-podge of the liturgy by
> substituting the Revised Standard Version, or some other contem-
> porary translation, for the reverent and stately King James Version
> in the Lessons (Epistle and Gospel) or even in other parts of the
> Liturgy. What a mess this would make.[10]

But in that very wholeness of the Common Service lay the seeds of
its own weakness. The use of the King James language exclusively was
too tight and confining, tying the English translation (and when its later
users forgot that it was a translation, tying the liturgy itself) to one time
and style.[11] The *Book of Common Prayer*, a product of evolving English,
was (and remains) more eclectic, taking its psalter from Coverdale and
its Epistles and Gospels and other scriptural quotations from the Great
Bible. It was an approach that was more adaptable.

Toward a Vernacular

By the middle of the twentieth century the hegemony of the Authorized Version had begun to break down as Reed had feared, and by the
end of the century there was no longer one commonly accepted translation of the Bible. That bond between classes and generations has been
dissolved. With it came a divergence in the language familiar to parents and their children. The language of the liturgy, like the language
of biblical translations, requires constant reworking to express ancient
meanings in contemporary language. What the parents say is not always
what the children hear. At Easter in 1986, to take one striking example, St. John's Episcopal Church in Northampton, Massachusetts, hung
a banner over its door proclaiming, "He is risen!" The Smith College
students across the street hung out their banner in reply: "She is rising." The people of St. John's wanted to placard their faith and to do

so used an ancient phrase, a scriptural quotation for those who recognized it (Matt. 28:6 and Mark 16:6 in the Authorized Version), familiar to them and hallowed by long use in Christianity. The college women, on the other side of the street, who read the banner in a quite different context, wanted to declare their own growing self-assurance. To some it was doubtless a distasteful challenge to the faith of the church; to others, including the newly installed president of Smith, it was an instructive confrontation of two cultures, two generations, two sensibilities. Reworking, explication, explanation, rethinking are constant necessities. St. John's would have done better to use the more specific and more traditional formulation, "Christ is risen." The Smith women rightly taunted the masculine pronoun in that setting and challenged the congregation to think again.

As early as the 1930s the Anglican liturgist W. H. Frere was open to the informed revision of the language of the liturgy:

> No one will deny that there is in English . . . a liturgical language which should be employed in corporate worship. The Prayer Book has created this. But it is not the same thing as Tudor English. Later epochs have contributed to it; and there is no reason why the twentieth century should not have a worthy contribution to make to it. Nor is there any reason why archaisms should be preserved when the meaning can equally well be expressed in intelligible and current but yet liturgical English.[12]

The interest in revision continued. The Second Vatican Council of the Roman Catholic Church hesitantly declared in its first document, promulgated December 4, 1963, "since the use of the mother tongue . . . may frequently be of great advantage to the people, the limits of its employment my be extended. This extension will apply in the first place to the readings and directives, and to some of the prayers and chants."[13] An article in the Lutheran journal *Una Sancta* in 1964 asked, "Shall We Use the Vernacular?" reflecting the remarkable and rapid movement in the Roman Church toward the language of the people. The Lutheran essay had in mind the vernacular modern English instead of the language of the Authorized Version that the Lutheran liturgies had carefully maintained.[14] The Standing Liturgical Commission of the Episcopal Church declared in 1966 that "there is no good reason to suppose that there is a single, proper 'style' of liturgical expression, much less any particular value in every Church's [i.e. denomination's] exhibiting the same 'style' in its liturgical vernacular."[15] Nonetheless, it recognized the desirability of some common formularies, especially texts such as the Lord's Prayer, the Creeds, the Gloria in Excelsis, and the Te Deum, "and doubtless the Psalter." Indeed, such texts have been made available through the work of the International Consultation on English Texts, published as *Prayers We Have in Common* (1970, 2d rev. ed. 1975) and are found in the service books of many denominations; and the 1979 *Book of Common Prayer* and the *Lutheran Book of Worship* share the same Psalter.

New Testament scholars and liturgists alike remind the church that no other language besides English has a distinctive grammatical form with which to address God and that what had become in English formulas of reverence and distance (thou, thy / thine, thee) were originally intended to convey closeness and intimacy, as is the custom still surviving among certain members of the Religious Society of Friends in conversing with one another. The church was reminded that Jesus taught his disciples to call the Most High *Abba*, "Daddy,"[16] suggesting the closeness of a family (Rom. 8:15–16). Tertullian in his treatise *On Baptism* (2) said that God's own properties are simplicity and power, and he noted that the very simplicity of God's means of working is a stumbling block to the earth-bound mind. Gregory of Nyssa in his *Address on Religious Instruction* (24) taught that the transcendent power of God is displayed not so much in the vastness of the heavens or the stars as in condescension to our weak nature. We marvel at the way "the sublime entered a state of lowliness." The mystery and greatness of God are revealed not in majesty and transcendence but in lowliness and human vesture in Christ and in the use of the simplest means, like water and bread and wine, to convey grace to us.[17]

Two fundamental facts of language need to be kept in mind as one considers the nature and care of the language of the liturgy. The first is that words, to say nothing of their connotations, change meaning as time passes, for language is alive, growing, and developing. Therefore to say the same thing one may need to say it differently in succeeding generations. A classic example in the English liturgy is the first word of the excellent prayer for guidance from the Gregorian sacramentary, as translated in the 1549 *Book of Common Prayer*:

> Prevent us, O Lord, in all our doings, with thy most gracious favor, and further us with thy continual help; that in all our works,

begun, continued, and ended in thee, we may glorify thy holy
Name, and finally, by thy mercy, obtain everlasting life; through
Jesus Christ our Lord.

"Prevent" derives from the Latin *praevenire*, to go before, to precede, but
that meaning and derivation are now lost to most speakers of English.
The opening of the prayer was changed in the 1789 American Prayer
Book therefore to "Direct us, O Lord, in all our doings, . . . " and it was
borrowed in this form for use in the service books of Lutherans and
others in America.

This change suggests a second fact of language that needs to be kept
in mind: a change in words, however slight, is a change in meaning,
however slight.[18] No alteration of words is ever harmless, any more than
any drug is without side effects. "Direct" in the collect is an acceptable
substitute for "prevent," but it changes the image. God is now seen to
be behind or above us, as it were, directing us in all our doings rather
than going ahead of us to prepare and to lead us in the way. Changing language must be done with sensitivity toward that living entity
by which we seek to communicate and with respect for the essence of
the faith that is to be preserved whole and entire and handed on to
succeeding generations.

The problem of liturgical language goes beyond the particular words
that are used. Many have suggested that a place to attack the problem of
communication of the being of God is the elimination of masculine pronouns and nouns associated with masculinity (he, his, him; Lord, King
Father).[19] But the liturgy is an action ("the work of the people"), something done rather than merely a text that is read, and attention to the
words alone is insufficient. Such attention may indeed be misleading,
even dangerous, if it suggests that changing the words of the liturgical
texts (which is easy enough to do) can replace strong and pointed sermons, careful instruction, and continuous education of clergy and laity
alike. New and altered texts cannot in themselves do the work of liturgical and spiritual renewal. They can never do the work of evangelism.

Formation by Fidelity

We must go behind troublesome words and particular images to a more
fundamental matter, the basic approach to liturgical worship. The pres-

ent essay is thus an exploration of the peculiar language of the liturgy, not to show how we can make it say what we mean (or what we want it to mean) but rather how we can and ought to mean what the liturgy at its best sets forth. Indeed, the most productive and rewarding approach to liturgy is to treat it as Luther teaches us to treat our neighbors,[20] "interpret charitably" (the older translation of the Catechism was "put the most charitable construction on") the words we hear and the actions we observe. One begins not by reforming the liturgy according to one's predilections but rather by being formed and informed by the great treasure of the church, a treasure perhaps second only to the Gospel itself (together with the needy who hear and receive it).[21]

Such is not a congenial approach these days. Neil Postman in his book *Amusing Ourselves to Death* has observed that this is a TV generation and that because television is basically entertainment we must therefore always be turning to something "new" with which to amuse ourselves.[22] That which requires careful and sustained attention, especially if it has been done for a long time, does not commend itself to such a generation of folks on the couch staring at the tube, with the remote in hand. This is not only a modern problem. It troubled Luther as well, and, in his characteristic unrestrained manner he reprimanded "those shallow-minded and disgusting spirits who blunder in like unclean pigs without faith or understanding, and who delight only in novelty and tire of it as quickly when it has worn off."[23]

Worship is a demanding discipline that has to do with the most profound experiences a human being can undergo: the fear, love, and trust that commingle when mortals confront the Holy One of Israel. Worship offers a glimpse of the divine majesty that lifts us out of the meanness of self-centered concerns toward a selfless offering of ourselves in praise, adoration, and service. It is not news that the church and its Bible are patriarchal. Undeniably, that tradition has at times and in ways perhaps not yet fully understood been oppressive, corrupting, and repressive to women and to men as well. To be sure, the church has in its long history much to be ashamed of, much to repent of. But in that long, complex, and varied story are also noble visions and stimulating approaches and revolutionary insights.[24] Without making light of pressing contemporary concerns, the argument of this book is that we first need to learn to attend to the still greater weight of the accumulated experience of the catholic church. There we will find resources to help us confront and overcome what are perceived as evils in our day and generation.

In the book of the prophet Jeremiah (6:16) the Lord God urges, "Stand at the crossroads, and look, and ask for the ancient paths, where the good way lies; and walk in it, and find rest for your souls." (The people's obstinate reply was "We will not walk in it.") Especially in times of the erosion of certainties there is comfort in walking in the ancient and enduring paths; but there is challenge there too, for in doing what has always (or at least long) been done we may not be doing what comes naturally. We are responding to a profound summons to a deeper, richer, grander life than we can conceive of on our own, the participation in a small way in the great work of remaking the world and reaching beyond this world of space and time into other dimensions that alone can satisfy the deepest longing of the human heart.

_____ *Chapter Two* _____

THE ENERGY OF LANGUAGE

L ITURGY SPRINGS from the creative energy of language. In the biblical understanding, this energy derives from the breath-spirit that
in the beginning formed and filled the creative word, "Let there be
light." Thus these energy-producing words are not merely human cre-
ations but a wonderful communication inspired by the Spirit of God.
In Christian terms, liturgy is ultimately the work of the Holy Spirit,
who, in the description given in Luther's *Small Catechism*, "calls, gathers, enlightens, and sanctifies the whole Christian church on earth, and
preserves it in union with Jesus Christ in the one true faith."[1]

A study of liturgy must inescapably consider language, including
metaphor and symbol, for language continues to echo and embody
those spirit-filled words, although their creative power may seldom be
apparent to the modern world. Words, we often assume, are frail, in-
substantial things, ultimately only wind, which, once spoken, are gone,
never to be recovered. They seem to be but breath losing itself in the
air. Even written words are often dismissed as "mere words." We are
continually deluged by such an unending torrent of words, spoken and
written, that we have learned not to listen attentively anymore. Most
of the words that engulf us seem not to mean very much.

More seriously, we have learned to distrust words. Language, it has
been argued, was a principal casualty of the First World War. Henry
James, interviewed by the *New York Times* in 1915 and reflecting on
recent casualty figures, remarked that "the war has used up words;
they have weakened, they have deteriorated like motor car tires;...we
are now confronted with a depreciation of all our terms, or, otherwise
speaking, with a loss of expression through an increase in limpness,
that may well make us wonder what ghosts will be left to walk."[2] Language was a principal casualty of the Great War. As a fearsome example,
Joachim C. Fest in his study *Hitler* (1974) notes that words had become
so cheap in Germany that even the most ominously brutal language

12

caused little alarm. Few people took Hitler at his word; too many failed to appreciate that here was one who not only talked about the coming "age of steel" and racial war but who would in fact in total war and the factories of death carry out precisely what he had promised. At the end of the resulting Second World War, George Orwell in the well-known essay "Politics and the English Language" warned against those who would drain meaning from plain words. By its continued manipulation as propaganda, language was being worn out. In the succeeding years we have seen too many advertisements, watched too many commercials, heard too many soporific speeches for us to maintain confidence in the power of words. But consider:

> I was sitting on a terrace ... reading and carding a modern novel, when a friend picked up my pile of cards and riffled through them. "Don't you sometimes," he asked, "wonder how many of the words you collect are worth having?"
>
> Naturally I told him off. Dictionary readers, I explained, weren't actuated by aesthetic or moral considerations, by quality or facility of communications. Their only duty was dispassionately to collect what had not yet been recorded or what supplements existing records.
>
> But I later thought about what he'd said. Why was it, I asked myself, that after an orgy of carding modern material I always felt a little depressed, perhaps arid or even soiled, and tended to seek refreshment by a spot of carding in George Eliot or in seventeenth-century laundry lists? It wasn't the *matter* that weighed me down; reviewers must soon learn to be almost impervious to the tone of the matter. It was, I decided, the cumulative effect of the collected words. Apparently words are something that can't, even with the coldest intentions in the world, be handled without emotional effect.[3]

Words, it appears, have inescapable vital power. They have an independent existence of their own, not entirely derived from those who utter them. Gertrude Stein, in a work called grandly *The Geographical History of America or the Relation of Human Nature to the Human Mind* (1936) told of how she discovered that "if you read with glasses and somebody is cutting your hair and so you cannot keep the glasses on and you use your glasses as a magnifying glass and so read word by word reading word by word makes writing that is not anything to be something."[4]

Spoken words are still more vigorous. Coleridge, who like his Ancient Mariner had "strange power of speech," was a compulsive talker. He observed, "Words are living powers, not merely articulated air";[5] they have a force, a life, almost a character and personality of their own. They partake of "an energy common to words and things, though embodied and controlled in words."[6] Such a profound understanding is far from the usual shallow notions of words and language, and such an understanding is essential for an understanding of liturgy.

Creation by Words

The creative power inherent in language[7] was clearly understood by all ancient peoples.[8] Throughout antiquity there was a common belief in the value and efficacy of words, which were believed to be operative realities. As early as perhaps 2850 B.C.E. there was an Egyptian myth, recorded in the much later document called the Memphite Theology, of creation by the power of the word: "Heart thought. Tongue spoke."[9] According to the Polynesian cosmogonic myth, Io (Iho), the supreme God of the Maori of New Zealand, separated the waters by the power of his words and created the sky and the earth.

> He began by saying these words, —
> That he might cease remaining inactive:
> "Light, become a darkness-possessing light."[10]

The cosmogonic words are creative words, charged with sacred power.[11] In 2 Esdras 6:6 creation is by the creator thinking his thoughts. In the translation of the Revised English Bible, "Then it was that I had my thought, and the whole world was created through me and through me alone."[12] The thought of creation seems here to be not only anterior but superior to the word by which creation was achieved. Northrop Frye understands this to be a later phase of language in which words become primarily the outward expression of inner thoughts or ideas. Subject and object are becoming more consistently separated; in the earlier phase, subject and object are not clearly separated.[13] As the Memphite Theology shows, thought and expression are seldom separated in cosmogonic myths.

The cosmogonic words of the mighty maker are creative words, charged with sacred power. Such words can be uttered by mortals whenever there is something to create, and they are included in magic formulae that are understood to do things, to accomplish what they were spoken to perform, with a power to cast spells and to remove spells. Cosmos-fashioning words are included in rituals to overcome and dispel darkness, to implant a child in a barren womb, to cheer a despondent heart, to shed light in secret places and matters, to gain inspiration in composing songs.[14] This understanding of the power of cosmogonic words is not merely a curiosity of ancient peoples. Even in Christianity, the service of readings in the Great Vigil of Easter begins with a reading of the account of creation from Genesis 1, as the renewal of the world by the death and resurrection of Christ is celebrated. The cosmos-creating words are renewed, and in Christ the universe begins again. "In the beginning" the Creator spoke the words; they are spoken again, and Christ the Word of God carries out the intention of the Creator. Such a sense of the creative power of language is not limited to the ancient and medieval world. Early in the twentieth century, a wise child, six and a half years old, told the Swiss psychologist Jean Piaget, "If there weren't any words, it would be very bad; you couldn't make anything."[15]

An indication of the power understood to be inherent in words is evident in the significance accorded to names throughout the ancient world. A name was much more than a convenient sign by which one could distinguish one person from another. A name was descriptive in a profound sense, for it was closely and intimately related to the character of the person who bore it. It was an expression of the person. The name was thought to be part of one's being and therefore was conceived of as possessing an infinitely greater degree of reality than a mere sign of identification. So we read that God has chosen the tabernacle "as a dwelling for his name" (Deut. 12:11). Throughout the Old Testament the name is a sort of double for the deity. God gave Aaron instructions for blessing the people and said that when the priests bestow God's blessing, "so they shall put my name on the Israelites, and I will bless them" (Num. 6:27). God says of the angel who guides the Israelites,"Be attentive to him and listen to his voice; do not rebel against him . . . for my name is in him" (Exod. 23:21). The verbal sign designating God is so charged with God's power and presence that it almost becomes God's self. The sign and the referent, the name and the person, cannot be separated. (Thus in the *Book of Common Prayer* and in previous Lutheran service books "Name" when it refers to God's Name is capitalized, for the Name is equivalent to the person.) In the New Testament too one can trace similar uses of the divine Name to stand for God's character, spirit, attitude, self. In the Fourth Gospel Jesus appropriates to himself divine titles such as Shepherd (Ezek. 34:11; John 10:11) and ultimately the divine Name itself, "I am" (Exod. 3:14; John 8:12, 58), shocking and offending many who heard him, for they clearly heard it for what it was — a claim to be God — and who therefore prepared to carry out the punishment for blasphemy prescribed in the Law and to stone the man from Nazareth.

This sense of the significance of a name comes from a profound awareness of the value and efficacy of words. In the Bible, "word" can mean that which is spoken ("the words of Jeremiah," a typical beginning of a prophetic book), but it can also mean a matter, an event, an act. Words, especially in ancient times, were believed to have a strong inherent power. A word is never an empty sound but an operative reality, the action of which cannot be hindered once it is pronounced.[16] "So shall my word be that goes out from my mouth; it shall not return to me empty, but it shall accomplish that which I purpose, and succeed in the thing for which I sent it" (Isa. 55:11). The divine word is always active in character and conversely God's action is always verbal in character.[17]

In Hebrew theology the word is substance, reality, an independent entity. The Hebrew word *dabar* is from the root meaning to get behind and to push; it is therefore "the projection forward of what lies behind," the translation into action of what is at first in the heart.[18] To separate especially God's thought from God's action, God's language from gesture, to the Hebrew mind would be unthinkable.

> In Hebrew thought a word was more than a sound expressing a meaning; a word actually did things. The Word of God is not simply a sound; it is an effective cause.... God's Word not only *said* things; it *did* things.[19]

God's word then is not only speech; it is also power.[20] Or, as Oscar Cullmann puts it, "Every creative self-revelation of God to the world happens through his word. *His word is the side of God turned toward the world.*"[21]

Dabar can mean in English both "word" and "event." The creative potency of the word is apparent in the familiar opening chapter of Genesis, in which God creates the cosmos through words: "God said, 'Let there be light'; and there was light." The prosaic language of the narrator of the creation account counterpoints the commanding tone of the divine speeches, "Let there be..."; "Day!" "Heaven!" "Earth!"[22] Echoing such an understanding of the creative potency of divine speech the psalmist declares,

> By the word of the Lord the heavens were made,
> and all their host by the breath of his mouth.
>
> (Ps. 33:6)

and

> For he spoke, and it came to be;
> he commanded, and it stood firm.
>
> (Ps. 33:9)

Such is the natural and expected consequence of the divine pronouncement: its utterance always abounds in creative power. The text is not to be read with surprise as if it witnessed to a wondrous miracle. Rather, creation followed naturally from the pronunciation of a word; God said the word, and it happened. That is the way it is with words, especially God's words; they have an energy and a power of their own.

Moreover, the creative words continue as God not only began but sustains and renews the creation.

> When you send forth your spirit, they are created;
> and you renew the face of the ground.
>
> (Ps. 104:30)

> Then they cried to the Lord in their trouble,
> and he saved them from their distress;
> he sent out his word and healed them,
> and delivered them from destruction.
>
> (Ps. 107:19–20)

> He sends out his command to the earth;
> his word runs swiftly.
> He gives snow like wool;
> he scatters frost like ashes.
> He hurls down hail like crumbs —
> who can stand before his cold?
> He sends out his word, and melts them;
> he makes the wind blow, and the waters flow.
>
> (Ps. 147:15–18)]

Speaking is accomplished by regulating the aspiration, and this is precisely how God created and renews the world: by breath that is both
God's spirit and God's word. "The divine word is always active in
character, and conversely God's action is always verbal in character."
    Such an understanding is not peculiar to the Hebrew Scriptures, as
we have seen. A Sumerian hymn sings,

> Thy word, a sublime net, stretches over heaven and earth, it falls
> on the sea, and the sea is rough, it falls on the cane plantation,
> and the cane sprouts, it falls on the waves of the Euphrates, the
> word of Marduk stirs up vast waves.[23]

As this hymn suggests, the divine word can be destructive as well as
creative.

> The voice of the Lord is over the waters;
>   the God of glory thunders,
>   the Lord, over mighty waters.
> The voice of the Lord is powerful;
>   the voice of the Lord is full of majesty.
> The voice of the Lord breaks the cedars;
>   the Lord breaks the cedars of Lebanon.
>
> The voice of the Lord shakes the wilderness;
>   the Lord shakes the wilderness of Kadesh.
> The voice of the Lord causes the oaks to whirl,
>   and strips the forest bare.
>   (Ps. 29:3–5, 8–9; see Jer. 1:9–10)

For the prophets, especially Jeremiah, the word has an objective and
dynamic character. The prophets are seized by a mysterious power that
sometimes crushes and tortures Jeremiah (Jer. 20:9) and that sometimes fills him with joy (Jer. 15:16). The word is always greater than
the prophet, who receives it only to transmit it; the prophet's function is simply to be a messenger who delivers the word. In the book of
Deuteronomy, the test of a true prophet, that is, one who speaks God's
words, is whether or not what the prophet says in fact happens (Deut.
18:13–22). If the prophet speaks with divine authority, speaking words
of creative force and power, the words must have their effect, and the
prophecy is confirmed.
    In the New Testament, too, words have power. In Luke's infancy nar-
rative we read, "Elizabeth . . . whom people called barren is now in her

sixth month, for nothing is impossible to God" (*ouk adunateisei para tou theou pan reima*, literally, "not impossible with God shall be the word/ matter/thing"; Genesis 18:14 in the Septuagint is similar). The phrase can be translated, as in the English Revised Version of 1881, "For no word of God shall be void of power" (Luke 1:37). The beginning of the Fourth Gospel, in a clear echo of the opening of Genesis, connects the creation with the Logos:

> In the beginning was the Word, and the Word was with God, and the Word was God. He was in the beginning with God. All things came into being through him, and without him not one thing came into being. (John 1:1–3)

Christ, the preexistent Logos, is the full realization and epitome of the plenitude of speech, a force with origins outside of time and prior to creation. The Nicene Creed affirms this creation by means of the second person of the Trinity: "through him all things were made." Throughout the Gospels the commands of Jesus echo the Creator's commands of power that made the universe: "Be opened" (Mark 7:34); "Lazarus, come out!" (John 11:43); "Young man, I say to you, rise!" (Luke 7:14); "Be silent, and come out of him!" (Mark 1:25); "He re- buked the winds and the sea; and there was a dead calm" (Matt. 8:26). Jesus, the Logos, is the creative power of God come to humanity, speak- ing not the word of knowledge but the word of power. He came not merely to say things but to do things for the world. His speaking was part of his doing. Even his words of teaching are often acted out in miracles. Indeed, he can bring the word only because he is the word.[24]

In the theology of the Fourth Gospel, the Logos is the fullest form of divine expression. The Logos performs certain functions: it judges, for hearing the truth always lays a responsibility on the hearer (John 12:48, "on the last day the word that I have spoken will serve as judge"); it purifies by exposing evil and indicating the good, by rebuking wrong and commending right ("You have already been cleansed by the word that I have spoken to you," John 15:3); it calls forth belief ("Many of those who heard the word believed," Acts 4:4); it is the agent of rebirth ("You have been born anew, not of perishable but of imperishable seed, through the living and enduring word of God," 1 Pet. 1:23). In Jesus the creative power of God comes to mortals, speaking not the word of knowledge but the word of power and authority (Heb. 1:3). He came to do things for his people.[25] It is not just that in Jesus God was acting to re-create the world, refashioning the creation described in Genesis 1, but in the anaphoric way of Scripture, history proceeds by a series of repetitions, returns, and echoes as the chain of saving events is woven intricately and solidly. The writer to the Hebrews declared:

> Long ago God spoke to our ancestors in many and various ways by the prophets, but in these last days he has spoken to us by a Son, whom he appointed heir of all things, through whom he also created the worlds. He is the reflection of God's glory and the exact imprint of God's very being, and he sustains all things by his powerful word. (1:1–3)

The pattern, moreover, is not occasional but continuous and without interruption. In Psalm 104:30,

> When you send forth your spirit they are created;
> and you renew the face of the ground,

one sees the close connection between speech and life. To separate language from action would be unthinkable because language is inescapably expression.

Human words partake of the indelible character of divine communication. Once spoken, they cannot be recalled, even when spoken in error.[26] Already set loose, they are released to do their work. So in a wonderfully dramatic and insightful passage, Isaac's mistaken blessing of Jacob (Gen. 27:18–40) cannot be revoked even though it was elicited by deception, for the words have been spoken. That is, they have been sent out to accomplish what they were spoken to achieve. All Isaac and Esau can do is stand helpless and shaken when the deception is revealed; Jacob has the blessing.[27] We know from our own experience that even unintentionally offensive words, once spoken, cannot be recalled. They have been released and have already begun their unpleasant work no matter how much we would have it otherwise. No apology, no matter how heartfelt, can cancel their poisoning effect.[28]

Moreover, words of mortals, like the words of God, can transform chaos into order. They too can be creative.

> A word has power in and of itself. It comes from nothing into sound and meaning; it gives origin to all things. By means of words can a man deal with the world on equal terms. And the word is sacred.[29]

N. Scott Momaday comments on the observation.

> When Aho [his grandmother] saw or heard or thought of some-
> thing bad, she said the word *zei-dl-bei*, "frightful." It was the one
> word with which she confronted evil and the incomprehensible. I
> liked to hear her say it, for she screwed up her face in a wonderful
> look of displeasure and clicked her tongue. It was not an excla-
> mation so much, I think, as it was a warding off, an exertion of
> language upon ignorance and disorder.[30]

Through language a spell is cast, a web is woven,[31] a world is created as
words call into being things that did not previously exist.

We know the triumph of a child who has learned a new word and
by it has gained a new power. When I had recently arrived in the
South Bronx as a young pastor, I attended the memorial service for Paul
Tillich in James Chapel of Union Theological Seminary. My wife and
son were inside, in the congregation; I waited outside in the vestibule
holding our year-and-a-half-old daughter, who found no reason to be
silent just because a great theologian was being solemnly remembered.
As she chattered and made noises, I held her and whispered again
and again, "Quiet!" "Quiet!" she replied brightly, as if to declare tri-
umphantly, "I can say that: Quiet!" And she repeated the word over
and over as we stood outside for the rest of the service. (I like to think
that Tillich would have been pleased at her discovery.)

Writers, particularly those who deal in the elevated and concentrated language of poetry, are discoverers who have found the right
words, and with that discovery comes a power. Poets are makers, for
"poet" derives from the Greek *poein*, to make, as Sir Philip Sidney noted
in his *Defense of Poesy* (1595). In the Renaissance in England there
were poets in the court of the king called the "courtly makers," specifically, court poets (often called "makers" in the sixteenth century both
in Scotland and England) of the reign of Henry VIII who introduced
the "new poetry" from Italy and France into English. Long before them,
Aristotle had understood the connection between poetry and making.
A work of the imagination is a creation, a creature, something alive
with its own life. All creative writers, but especially the oldest and most
persistent, the poets, by their imagination breathe life into the dust.
"Imagination does not arise from the environment but has the power to
create it!" Louise Levertov declared.[32]

In 1988 Salmon Rushdie's novel *The Satanic Verses* brought down upon him the enmity of much of the Muslim world and a *fatwa*, a death sentence, from the Ayatollah Khomeini forcing Rushdie into hiding for his life. Those who reacted so violently to what they saw as blasphemy may have been acting in part out of a world view, alien to present Western culture, in which words are the equivalent of actions. For example, before the civil marriage laws were enacted, a man could divorce his wife simply by saying three times, "I divorce you." Many Westerners could not understand the hostility that the novel had generated, because they said, "It is only fiction." But language is never so innocuous. This is not, however, to condone censorship.[33] In his powerfully argued tract for liberty of publication John Milton argued in 1644,

> Books are not absolutely dead things, but doe contain a potencie of life in them to be as active as that soule was whose progeny they are. . . . [A]s good almost kill a Man as kill a good Book; who kills a Man kills a reasonable creature, Gods Image; but hee who destroyes a good Booke, kills reason it selfe, kills the Image of God, as it were in the eye. Many a Man lives a burden to the Earth; but a good Booke is the pretious lifeblood of a master spirit, imbalm'd and treasur'd up on purpose to a life beyond life. 'Tis true, no age can restore a life, whereof perhaps there is no great losse; and revolutions of ages do not oft recover the losse of a rejected truth, for the want of which whole Nations fare the worse. We should be wary therefore what persecution we raise against the living labours of publick men, how we spill that season'd life of man preserv'd and stor'd up in Books; since we see a kinde of homicide may be thus comitted, sometimes a martyrdome.[34]

A primitive power lurks in language, and that living power lies at the heart of thought itself. Jacques Maritain wrote that a sign "makes something other than itself present to knowledge."

> The discovery of language, then, coincides with the discovery of the relation of signification, and this would explain why, as a matter of fact, the invention of language and the birth of ideas, the first release of the intellect's power, probably took place at the same time.[35]

Thinking and language are inseparable. A wordless thought seems impossible.[36]

Language and Gesture

Language, as R. P. Blackmur noted in 1952, involves gesture; his essay was called "Language as Gesture." Blackmur begins with the obvious remark, "Language is made of words, and gesture is made of motion." Then he puts the statement the other way round, which is more arresting. "Words are made of motion, and gesture is made of language." Words are made of an action or response at whatever remove, and gesture is made of language beneath or beyond or alongside of the language of words. His thesis is that "when the language of words most succeeds it *becomes* gesture in its words."[37] A few years later John Searle began to speak of speech-acts, performative words that do not simply describe or communicate existing situations but that create new situations.[38] Such language is usually accompanied by ritual actions such as making a promise and shaking hands, christening a ship, conferring academic degrees. Liturgical language also creates new situations. Liturgy is composed of conjunctions of sights and sounds, words and actions, that function as avenues of divine service — of both God's service to us and our service to God.[39] Another way of saying this is to say that Christian worship is not just words but word and sign, or in a still more familiar expression, word and sacrament. Liturgical language therefore consists of sensible and sensuous words and signs together, for the words, especially the words of the liturgy, are active, performative words,[40] which do not simply describe or communicate existing situations but which create new situations. The words of the liturgy are speech-acts, which have to do not with expressing private thoughts but with social interaction. In liturgical speech one sees and hears and feels: "John, I baptize you..."; "Mary, child of God, you have been sealed..."; "I forgive you all your sins"; and, in still larger language and gesture, "This is my body." Thus a liturgy is more than a text. A liturgical text may be compared to the script of a drama; when one reads and examines only the script, the event of the drama, its performance, is seriously diminished, for the action is absent, the movement is missing. In the liturgy, accompanying the words and the text, supporting and enhancing them, are gesture, action, movement.

The liturgy may be understood as a species of drama, combining words and movement. In older forms of the liturgy, still practiced in some places in Christianity, when the altar was near the east wall of the chancel and the ministers presided facing the same way as the people, toward the altar as representatives of the congregation, the formalized dance movements of the liturgical action were especially apparent.[41] A solemn high mass began with a formalized and highly refined entrance rite. The three sacred ministers (celebrant in the center, deacon to the right, subdeacon to the left) approached the altar and genuflected in unison before it. A thurible was given to the celebrant, who honored the altar with incense, moving from the center to the right, incensing the inner part of the mensa, the right end of the altar, across the front part of the mensa; then the inner part of the mensa to the left was censed, the left end of the altar, the front part of the mensa, then the whole front of the altar as the celebrant moved across to the right corner again; all the while the deacon walked beside the celebrant to the right and the subdeacon to the left. At the right corner of the altar where the missal rested, the three ministers formed a line, the celebrant on the footpace of the altar, the deacon on a step or two down, and the subdeacon a step or two lower still. After the Introit and as the Kyrie concluded, the three moved, still in a line, to the center of the altar where the celebrant intoned the first phrase of the Gloria in Excelsis. The deacon and the subdeacon came up to stand on their respective sides of the celebrant for the canticle. As it concluded, the deacon and subdeacon formed a line behind the celebrant and as the celebrant turned toward the congregation for the salutation before the collect, they moved a few paces aside, the deacon moving to the right and the subdeacon to the left, to give the celebrant and congregation an unimpeded view of each other. They then reformed the line and moved together to the right corner, where the book was, for the collect. The celebrant and deacon then moved to their chairs to the right of the altar and sat down while the subdeacon read the Epistle. And so throughout the mass, the three sacred ministers moved in carefully prescribed, practiced, and graceful patterns, their movements enhancing the actions of the liturgy, proclaiming the harmony of the church in which all of the members do not have the same office but in which all have responsibility. Bewildering in its complexity to those unfamiliar with it, the richness of the movements is nonetheless a sign of the harmonious diversity of the whole church.

In the medieval church a sense of the creative energy of words remained. Words were always accompanied by actions. Indeed, the primacy of action was so firmly maintained that the sermon was often omitted altogether at mass. To pause for what seemed an interruption of the action by a sermon seemed undesirable. Words required one to do things, and the active words of the mass had a forward-driving energy that could not rest until the ritual had been completed.

The liturgical renewal of the latter twentieth century involved a recovery of the clarity and depth of the central signs of the church's faith and worship. The principal sign is now understood to be the gathering of the Christian assembly, and of central importance to that gathering is the book and the bath and the meal: the reading and proclamation of Holy Scripture, the mystery of water that drowns and washes and enlivens, the significance of eating with Christ and with one another in a foretaste of the feast to come.

In liturgical action, not all gesture needs to be or should be accompanied by words. Sometimes the act itself is sufficiently powerful, for gesture is a statement.[42] Gestures, movements, and actions speak a powerful language to those with eyes to see. The sign of the cross made over a person or an object, without any words, effectively conveys a blessing. A bow made to an altar or to a cross expresses reverence; words need not be said. In the Roman Catholic ordination rites the bishop lays his hands on the head of the ordinand in silence. The gesture is an expression of prayer for consecration by the Holy Spirit; the ordination prayer follows. The silent gesture and the spoken words together constitute the act of ordination. In the Lutheran revision of the liturgy in preparation for the *Lutheran Book of Worship* of 1978, the action of breaking the bread, a widespread custom, was introduced and words recalling Luke 24:35 were added to the action, "When we eat this bread we share the body of Christ." Then an analogous action was created, lifting the cup, an act altogether without purpose or meaning, with accompanying words,"When we drink this cup we share the blood of Christ." Then, equal time having been given to both bread and cup, even though only the bread needed anything done to it, the congregation was given a prayer to say, "Reveal yourself to us, O Lord, in the breaking of bread, as once you revealed yourself to the disciples."[43] This complex of actions came to be seen by most as the redundancy it was, and in the *Lutheran Book of Worship* the fraction is simply directed by the rubrics, "The bread may be broken for distribution." (In the Notes on the Liturgy the words from the preparatory booklet are preserved for those who could not let them go.[44])

Commentary on liturgical action, made outside the ritual, can be helpful, suggesting new insights, revealing that which is unseen and unfelt by some participants, articulating that which sensitive celebrants know. But words within a ritual explaining the actions occur only when a rite becomes opaque. They represent an attempt at pumping life into that which is dying or injecting meaning into that which has but recently been devised. The cathodes of explanatory words may be applied, but the monster does not walk. Certain gestures should not have accompanying words, especially words of explanation that say in effect, "this means such and such." A gesture is made, and those who see it should be able to read in it the meaning of the sign. "The liturgical act can be realized by looking," wrote Romano Guardini. "This does not mean that the sense of vision takes note of what is going on in front, but it is itself a living participation in the act." The faithful "should see the inner sense of the outward sign," without which the actions would be a waste of time and energy; it would be better simply to say what was meant. The gestural symbol, however, is the expression of the inward through the outward, "and must as such be co-performed through the act of looking."[45] What is required is to really look, to see with understanding. Such learning is actually a rediscovery of what we already know, for gesture, as St. Augustine noted, is "the natural language of all peoples."[46] The assembly, the foremost gesture of the Christian community, is their central liturgical symbol as they gather from diverse places to perform their liturgy with water, a book, and bread and wine.

Language can be devalued and its creative energy dissipated. The printed page tames some of the vividness and energy of the spoken word. Walter Ong has suggested that in an oral culture, sound pours into the hearer and that knowledge is something external, enacted, unifying.[47] In a literate culture, on the other hand, sight depends on and establishes a certain distance, keeping viewer and viewed apart. For the practice of liturgy, the living experience of the performative speech-acts is deadened through excessive dependence on printed texts, by presiding ministers who have not memorized but have to read the Apostolic Greeting ("The grace of our Lord Jesus Christ, the love of God, and the communion of the Holy Spirit be with you all"), the salutation before the prayer of the day ("The Lord be with you"), the dialogue at the beginning of the Great Thanksgiving; and by congregations who must read their simple responses ("And also with you"; "We lift them to the Lord," "It is right to give him thanks and praise," "Amen") and who must follow on a leaflet the proclamatory reading of the Scriptures. The written word has become for us the basic form of language, not a secondary vehicle for its communication. "So tied are we to the written or printed page that we have lost any awareness of the orality of language, let alone of reading. Not only do we want everything of moment 'in black and white,' but we presume that it is the fundamental medium of language."[48]

Television, it may be observed, has undermined the literate character of the culture, and in an electronic age sound again pours into the hearer and viewer as something external, enacted, and unifying. The distance emphasized by print is no longer as great as it once seemed, and modern culture may again be ready to respond to the living energy of words and gestural acts.

The Role of Silence

The ancient and continuing profound respect for the power of language involves inescapably an equally profound respect for silence, without which the sounds are a meaningless jumble. Rests in music, spaces in architecture, pauses in poetic lines are as important as the notes, the masses, and the articulated syllables. Indeed, it is the silences as much as the sounds that enliven the metronome by animating with rhythm the variations of the meter.[49]

It is, however, more than merely a matter of rhythm, of alternation and contrast. As primal peoples understood, there is a creative potency in silence and solitude. Indeed, it is Josef Pieper's thesis that the basis of culture is to be found in the restfulness afforded by leisure. The Latin *schola,* school, the place where we teach and educate, he points out, derives from the Greek *skolē,* leisure.[50] There are two parts of a whole culture; there is work with its activity, and there is leisure with its non-activity, inward calm, silence. In contrast to work and business, leisure is not being busy but letting things happen. It is the alternative to work and thus makes daily routine meaningful. It gives direction and coherence to the workaday world by paying attention to what is real, lasting, ennobling.

> Leisure is a form of silence, of that silence which is the prerequisite of the apprehension of reality: only the silent hear and those who do not remain silent, do not hear. Silence, as it is used in this context, does not mean 'dumbness' or 'noiselessness'; it means

more nearly that the soul's power to 'answer' to the reality of the
world is left undisturbed. For leisure is a receptive attitude, a contemplative attitude, and it is not only the occasion but also the
capacity for steeping oneself in the whole of creation.[51]

Erich Fromm, commenting on the meaning of the Sabbath, observes
that the weekly day of rest is the one day on which human work is
not permitted to disturb the order of nature. On the Sabbath the world
runs without human interference, a sign of the promised harmony of
all creation.[52] The silence of the Sabbath is thus a sign of completion
and fulfillment, in contrast to the dark void of the primordial silence
with which the Genesis account begins. The first silence is the emptiness that precedes time; the second silence is the repose and calm that
sanctifies it.[53]

Even the people's work of liturgy requires times of silence to attend
to the deepest meanings of what is happening. The silence is a willingness to listen, to hear, to be led into truth. Silence within a liturgical
action teaches patience and encourages tolerance. It is a willingness to
listen to what is taking place rather than impose a meaning on it, an
open spirit willing to be submerged in a sometimes alien activity. More
than an empty or even a pregnant pause, silence too is a prayer, an
expression of listening, of waiting, of being receptive. It is the cessa-
tion of those inner voices that would respond too quickly, in advance
of listening, thereby destroying receptivity. Silence is finally communal
as is evident in the meeting for worship of the Religious Society of
Friends. Each one present is not engaged in an isolated activity car-
ried out within the individual mind and spirit. Rather, each is part of
a corporate activity, the characteristic silence, a shared receptivity that
is more than one can experience alone. This attitude of receptive attention, letting things happen, is more evident in the services of Daily
Prayer than in the Eucharist. The Eucharist is largely movement, action,
events — found even in the dynamic of the sermon — with a purposeful
direction: gathering, proclaiming and listening, bringing gifts, sharing a
meal, scattering to "serve the Lord." The Daily Office, on the other
hand, is primarily meditative and non-directional, joining, insofar as
mortals can, the praise offered by the cosmos to the Creator. But both
foci of the church's worship, Eucharist as well as Daily Prayer, require
and ought to encourage and facilitate the receptive attitude that can
apprehend the depths of reality.

In the third of thirty-eight "Tentative (First Model) Definitions of Poetry" prefaced to *Good Morning, America,* Carl Sandburg defined poetry as "the report of a nuance between two moments, when people say 'Listen!' and 'Did you see it?' 'Did you hear it?' 'What was it?' "[54] In the silence of the liturgy one hears the poetry of revelation, the echoes of deepest meaning, and a liturgy must allow times of silence (after the lessons, after the sermon, after the reception of the Holy Communion) for the meanings to reverberate in the hearts of the participants.

There are, moreover, times and occasions when words fail. Profound revelation is wordless. In the familiar words of Phillips Brooks's Christmas carol:

> How silently, how silently,
> The wondrous gift is given;
> So God imparts to human hearts
> The blessings of his heaven.

Behind the thought of that lovely hymn lie the more ancient words of the Liturgy of St. James as versified by Gerald Moultrie:

> Let all mortal flesh keep silence
> And with fear and trembling stand,
> Ponder nothing earthly minded,
> For with blessing in his hand
> Christ our God to earth descendeth,
> Our full homage to demand.

Fulfilling ancient words and begetting endless words of praise and reflection and proclamation, the Incarnation itself was wordless. "The Word within a word, unable to speak a word," as Launcelot Andrewes preached and T. S. Eliot recalled.[55] The Revelation of St. John the Divine describes the opening of the final seal of the scroll: "When the Lamb opened the seventh seal, there was silence in heaven for about half an hour" (Rev. 8:1). Words can dilute the direct appropriation of the gifts of God.

Those who have passed beyond the realm of language are not thereby in a void.

Wherever the word is revered as a tool around which still vibrates the magic halo of primeval creation, there silence, too, is esteemed a reservoir of spiritual strength.[56]

It is out of the pool of silence that words come forth, and it is back into that silence that they return when they have accomplished their work. An African formula at the end of a story, respectful of this mystery, declares, "I put the tale back where I found it."[57] The silent source of speech is at least as important as the creative, energetic words themselves: "Meaning is what silence does when it gets into words."[58] Silence complements the finitude of sound with the grace of infinity, creating a satisfying wholeness.[59] When the value of words deteriorated, the intrinsic meaning of silence was also lost. It is not surprising, therefore, that one of the principal discoveries in the renovation of the liturgy in the twentieth century has been the value of periods of silence.

The strident certainties that some would impose on us are countered by the often neglected "doctrine of reserve — the preservation of a sense of reverence and awe in the face of the mystery of God."[60] It is a mystery so profound and indeed so terrifying that respectful Jews refrain from even pronouncing the divine Name. The God of the Bible, who makes contact with mortals and who is involved in the events of history, nonetheless remains unfathomable. God remains the hidden God, *deus absconditus* (Isa. 45:15). Human resources and earthly language reach their limits when they attempt to understand Infinitude.[61]

Words of prayer and devotion bring us to the edge of eternity, and there they dissolve. The incomprehensible invites us to partake of its mystery. Expounding Psalm 147 (146 in Hebrew and English numbering), St. Augustine declared,

> Let human voices be still and mortal thinking be silent. They should strive toward what is incomprehensible not as if they were going to comprehend, but as if they were going to participate.[62]

For all of their marvelous creative energy, the words of devotion cannot finally comprehend their grand subject.

> Words strain,
> Crack and sometimes break, under the burden,
> Under the tension, slip, slide, perish,
> Decay with imprecision, will not stay in place,
> Will not stay still

lamented T. S. Eliot.[63] It is another recognition that words are living creatures. Samuel Johnson opined:

Poetical devotion cannot often please.... Contemplative piety, or the intercourse between God and the human soul, cannot be poetical. Man admitted to implore the mercy of his Creator and plead the merits of his Redeemer is already in a higher state than poetry can confer.[64]

Like the language of poetry, the language of prayer is occupied with the frontiers of consciousness beyond which words fail, although meanings still exist.[65] Silence is a recognition and acknowledgement of the limits of language, an affirmation of the transcendent splendor of God, and an expression of a willingness to be led into it.

Chapter Three

POETRY:
ALLUSIVE LANGUAGE

~ ✚ ~

I N THE SECOND of his *Four Quartets*, "East Coker," T. S. Eliot gives
the encouragement and warning, "If you do not come too close, if
you do not come too close / On a summer midnight you can hear the
music." The music of which Eliot writes is a fragile and delicate thing
that can be missed by the brash and insensitive and be destroyed by
analysis, but to those with ears to hear it is lovely and compelling. G. K.
Chesterton noted, "Mysticism keeps men sane. As long as you have
mystery you have health; when you destroy mystery you create morbid-
ity. The ordinary man has always been sane because the ordinary man
has always been a mystic. He has permitted the twilight."[1]

If there is such a thing as a religious view of the world it is simply that there are no such things as ordinary, straightforward actions.
Every action, every object is fraught with meaning, much of which
is not apparent. Religion is the awareness of more dimensions, more
depth, more importance, more significance than that which appears
on the surface. Religion suggests an awareness of and attention to the
transcendent, which may paradoxically be incarnate and close at hand,
although unnoticed.

Lyric Brevity

Lyric poetry is a good starting place for the study of poetry in general,
and poetry is a good starting place for the study of religion and especially of liturgy. The brevity of the lyric form invites and encourages
close attention to each word and also to the order of those words, for in
the concentrated and allusive richness of the language many wonderful
things are happening.

A lyric is a song that breaks out when one is suddenly aware of a new facet, a new dimension, a new layer of experience, and the song provides a new understanding and a new, although perhaps temporary, control of that awareness. A lyric is reasonably simple and uncomplicated; "the lyric impulse... is for simplicity both in words and in thought."[2] In form the lyric is small, unambitious, polished,[3] a poem that "takes one thing at a time,"[4] brief and straightforward, yet carefully done and therefore worthy of careful attention. In theme, the lyric derives from emotional commonplaces,[5] those experiences we all share: love, death, war, the natural world. In sound, the lyric is a "still, small voice" of charm and grace, which often goes unheard amid the pandemonium of the world and its politics, economics, business, and industry. No one lyric depends on another for worth or meaning; each is complete in itself, a whole entity. The lyric presents a self-contained creation, a small, unified world, an ordered creation distinct from the confused and confusing multiplicity that surrounds us. Lyric poetry isolates feeling in a small compass and thus renders it at its most intense. Its concentrated expression of feeling does not provide a story or an explanation, just feeling alone, clarified, articulated, and transformed from privacy to publicity.[6]

These relatively uncomplicated songs open up to us a new appreciation of the essential role of poetry in human experience. It is not an optional decoration that can be added, if one is so inclined, after one has taken care of the necessities of life. Poetry was there from the beginning of civilization: it is as ancient as humanity itself. Poetry is so basic because song gives us a way to break out of our inarticulateness.[7] Most of us suffer from a natural yet painful inability to overcome dumbness. We want to speak, but we cannot. We believe that we have something to say, but we cannot find a way to say it. In ancient times and well into the development of Western civilization, it was believed that all nature upon occasion found a voice, and rocks and trees as well as animals broke into song. A fourth-century Christmas hymn by Prudentius (348–413), in John Mason Neale's translation "Of the Father's Love Begotten," calls upon every earthly tongue to join the angelic chorus in praising the incarnate God:

> O ye heights of heaven adore him;
> Angel hosts, his praises sing;
> Powers, dominions, bow before him,
> And extol our God and King;

> Let no tongue on earth be silent,
> Every voice in concert ring,
> Evermore and evermore.[8]

A sixth-century Easter hymn by Fortunatus (530–609) understands that all creatures, all creation joins to praise the resurrected king:

> Earth with joy confesses, clothing her for spring,
> All good gifts return with her returning King:
> Bloom in every meadow, leaves on every bough,
> Speak his sorrow ended, hail his triumph now.
>   'Hell today is vanquished, heaven is won today!'
>
> Months in due succession, days of lengthening light,
> Hours and passing moments praise thee in their flight;
> Brightness of the morning, sky and fields, and sea,
> Vanquisher of darkness bring their praise to thee:
>   'Welcome, happy morning! age to age shall say.'[9]

A seventh-century Greek hymn by St. Germanus (ca. 634–734), echoing the psalms (see 148:2, 9; 98:7–8), is even more explicit. Angels sing the newborn Savior, then the earth joins in, then mortals:

> While thus they sing your Monarch
> Those bright angelic bands,
> Rejoice, ye vales and mountains!
> Ye oceans, clap your hands.
>
> Since all he comes to ransom,
> By all be he adored,
> The Infant born in Bethlehem,
> The Savior and the Lord![10]

There is in these lines an allusion to the redemption of all creation — valleys, mountains, and oceans as well as all mortal flesh — through the sacrifice of Christ, the maker, monarch, and redeemer of the whole world. Fortunatus's great passion hymn "Sing, My Tongue the Glorious Battle" (*Pange, lingua, gloriosi proelium certaminis*) likewise tells of the cleansing of the physical world by the blood shed on the cross: "Earth and stars and sky and ocean / By that flood from stain are freed"[11] (see Rom. 8:19–23). In such impressive pictures we are surrounded by created things struggling to break into song. In the words of Maltbie Davenport Babcock's familiar hymn, "All nature sings, and round me rings / The music of the spheres."[12] The incessant and surrounding music is both audible (wind and birds and brooks) and inaudible (the harmonious sounds of the heavenly spheres described in Pythagorean astronomy). To be sure, humanity does not always sing. In theological terms, sin is the reason why singing is so rare. But despite sin, in joy, in pain, in triumph, in sorrow the human spirit sometimes wells up in an irrepressible urge to sing.

There is in any song "an element of instinctive spontaneity."[13] We all share the instinct, but not many of us are singers, poets, composers. Each lyric begins with raw experience, life as it impinges upon us, and that experience is rather chaotic. Then we transform that raw experience into significant experience by breaking it, selecting and discarding elements of it, expanding and examining others so that by this transformation a purified experience, purged of its rudeness, emerges.[14]

The urge to sing and make poetry and to tell stories is no decorative addition to the meaningful life of humanity. It is at its very center, the essence of what makes us human. It is the driving force of civilization pushing us from chaos to order, from experience to meaning. Poetry applies words to our situations, to the conditions of being in which we find ourselves. By doing so it gives us pleasure because it helps us articulate our states of mind.[15] The poets we value are important because they speak for us with words we could never find and they help us learn to speak for ourselves. Poets find the right words and arrange them in the right order for what "we already dimly and dumbly feel, and they also fertilize in our consciousness responses which were lying inert and cloddish."[16] John Keats observed that "Poetry should strike the Reader as a wording of his own highest thoughts and appear almost a remembrance."[17] In Robert Frost's oft-quoted remark, "For me the initial delight is in the surprise of remembering something I didn't know I knew."[18] Poetry makes explicit many thoughts and considerations which are so closely connected with action that they are almost part of it, and become conscious only when the right words are found for them.

Art is not an imitation but a discovery of reality.[19] No poet can create an entirely new language. The poet has to adopt words and has to respect the fundamental rules of language. But to the familiar words and grammar the poet gives not only a new turn but a new life and by a metamorphosis transforms our common words into a new and fresh creation. In this sense a great poet speaks a language that has never been heard before and that never repeats itself. It is a new and fresh creation.[20] Poets speak for us, and they help us learn to speak for ourselves, charging with new meaning all our common words.

Because we cannot comprehend or express the overwhelming density of experience, all use of language must necessarily be a limitation, for we cannot take in all that is impinging upon us each second, overwhelming our senses. Careful language and especially poetry gives concentration and precision. But this precision induces expansion as one word leads to another, and composition facilitates discovery. The increased and heightened sensitivity finds an outlet in song.

> Song not only relieves the pressure of the emotions but makes explicit many thoughts and considerations which are so closely connected with action that they are almost part of it, and become conscious only when the right words are found for them.[21]

In social life, custom, the embodiment of accumulated experience, has the weight of age and authority; but if custom is not exposed to new forces "sufficiently powerful to insist on concessions being made to them, custom breeds its own dangers."[22] Then custom "lives on its own resources and may elaborate them from within instead of looking beyond or outside them, especially in anything to do with the supernatural and the unseen, but in the essential task of struggling to keep alive it restricts and forbids novelty and invention." Therefore, the "mystery which provokes song into being and enthralls us through it"[23] is not only powerful but necessary for the advance of humanity and of civilization.

In ancient societies song rises from rhythmical action; words are added to give a new clarifying element. T. S. Eliot observed:

> I believe that the properties in which music concerns the poet most nearly, are the sense of rhythm and the sense of structure.
> ... I know that a poem, or a passage of a poem, may tend to realize itself first as a particular rhythm before it reaches expression in words, and that this rhythm may bring to birth the idea and the image; and I do not believe that this is an experience peculiar to myself.[24]

The words that arise from the rhythm are essentially dramatic. Ancient song takes its singers out of themselves by making them act a part, giving that distance from the immediate scene that is the foundation of all the arts and giving the detachment that enables humanity to look at themselves or their circumstances from other motives than the need or impulse to perform a certain action.[25] Song is therefore a communal activity. It is also a necessary activity through which those "who might otherwise give in to the malice of circumstances, find their old powers renewed or new powers stirring in them, and through these life itself is sustained and renewed and fulfilled."[26]

It is sometimes suggested that liturgy is poetry, but if that is so, then the liturgy is poetry in its most ancient and primeval sense, compressed and evocative words that are sung and danced. Words and melody and movement are wedded, each incomplete without the other.[27] To examine only the text of a liturgy is like studying only the words of an ancient lyric. The melody and the movement are missing, and so two-thirds of the experience is lost. The ancient understanding of the vigor of words and language naturally issues in the connection of words with music and dance to display and perform the vibrancy of speech.

In most primitive song, words are only part of a complex unity. They are in the first place sung, sometimes accompanied, sometimes not, and the singing is often joined to some kind of action, which may be a dance, illustrating what the words say and making their references more forceful, or may be only supporting actions such as clapping or stamping the feet to express the energy felt in the words.[28] Words, music, and movement present a single entity. Nonetheless, even without the music and the action, the words can take us into the consciousness at its most excited or concentrated moments.[29]

Liturgy ("the work of the people") has affinities with drama ("a thing done"). Both have an essential quality of enactment; both are a form of imitative action. The text of each is like the score of a symphony: a finished work, yet only a potentiality until it is performed. So every performance, even by the same actors, represents a different realization of its possibilities, and no single performance can fully realize all of its possibilities.[30] The mode of liturgy, like drama, is selective and intensive, and by selecting and intensifying examples the liturgist and the dramatist can illuminate the whole. The liturgy highlights those parts of the story of humanity that have been found formative by the Christian tradition, events that have been experienced as revelatory. They show that the story of humanity is in fact the story of God.

The Role of the Reader

Many ancient songs are remarkably brief, both in thought and in words. Like the little song of the well given in Numbers 21:17–18,[31] like ancient Native American poetry and song, like the fragments collected in the *Greek Anthology,* they are mere wisps of song, not entirely complete in themselves. The singer sketches a thought or impression, and it is left to the poetic imagination of the listeners and their resources of mythic knowledge to supply the gradations of color and mythical context. The listeners are themselves poets who cooperate with the singer and fill in the sketch to completeness. There is an "inside song" that goes on within the hearers, stirred by these few words. "The song is so short because we know so much," explained a Native American woman to a bewildered inquirer.[32] Thus poetry is a more common enterprise and possession in ancient cultures than modern people are accustomed to. It is a communal activity: singer and hearers are partners in the creation.

To learn to respond to the exact use of words is to learn to read with the attention and intensity necessary to claim their music for oneself.[33] The poetry of the Native Americans and of the *Greek Anthology* can help us see the power of language. Much of this poetry is fragmentary. The *Greek Anthology* collects many remnants, and the Native American poetry, one needs to remember, is only part of a whole experience of words and music and dance. Nonetheless, this poetry can be useful precisely because it is so brief. These little poems of few words force readers to examine them closely and carefully, encouraging readers to feel the individual words intensely. Such poetry is deceptive in its simplicity. Its very brevity invites careful examination. Why this word? Why concentrate on this simple action? Why is this simple observation taken as a subject? What depths lie behind each significant word?

An instructive example is this song from the Colorado River Basin:

> The deer
> looks at a flower.[34]

That's all there is to it. It is simple, easy to parody. "The professor stands on the floor." "The student sits in the chair." But is the parody equal to the original? Why a deer? Why a flower? Why both in one poem? What similarities are there between them? What contrasts? Why should there be an attraction of one to the other? The deer: a living creature, graceful and handsome, solid and strong, sizeable, colored so as to be hidden in the woods, free to move through the woodland, sentient. A flower: also alive, graceful and beautiful, but delicate and fragile, small, colored so as to attract attention, rooted in one place, without the same sentient faculty as the deer. The deer with the ability to see looks at the flower, the higher order of nature looking down literally and figuratively at a lower order, which is no less beautiful. The deer stands between the human and the flower in the chain of being. Can the deer, we may perhaps wonder, respond to the delicate beauty of the flower? The poem suggests it, but makes no commitment. A human sees the scene and makes a song of it. A person looks at the deer looking at the flower. The interaction expands as the complex relationships and interdependence of nature subtly unfold. The deer links the human and the flower, yet the singer sees both the deer and the flower and the relationships between them. Moreover, as the deer looks at the flower in the song, so the audience looks at the singer who is also a source of beauty. The syllogism is suggested:

audience : singer :: deer : flower

A tiny incident. Yet as Donald Hall reminded us in his wise book *Writing Well*, "Nothing understood is trivial."[35]

The Omaha tribal prayer

Wa-kon'da
here needy he stands
and I am he[36]

is a pleasantly indirect appeal to god. Instead of an urgently direct request such as the insistent cry of the Christian liturgy, "Lord, have mercy," the Omaha in a kind of intercession calls Wa-kon'da's attention to a needy person standing before him, and then, having accomplished that, the singer identifies himself with that needy person. The prayer is a notable achievement of delicate perspective and quiet humility.

Another body of brief, even fragmentary, poems that require close attention to their carefully crafted language is found in the *Greek Anthology*. The collection dates from the tenth century of the common era, but the lyrics flourished from the middle of the seventh century to the end of the sixth century B.C.E. In perhaps the best-known Greek epitaph, Simonides wrote simply and movingly of the dead at Thermopylae,

> Traveller, take this word to the men of Lakedaimon:
> We who lie buried here did what they told us to do.[37]

The fallen ask the traveller ("stranger" in the Greek, someone the dead have never met), one who is free to move about, to carry for them the message back to their superiors in Sparta that the dead lie fallen having obeyed the code of their city. They had acted as Spartans had been brought up to act. It is poem first of all of obedience and faithfulness, of pride in having done one's duty, even in death. But one cannot say that without implying a judgment on that code of precepts which required them to spend their lives in obedience to laws that they could not understand, and a judgment upon those whose orders resulted in the destruction of young lives. But the poem is delicately balanced between pride and judgment, and neither is quite what is said. Rather, it is a mixture that will not let us see and feel the one without the other. Such is war. Such is life. And therein lies the poignancy of the inscription. Moreover, the relationship between the dead and the travelling stranger is complex. The command "take this word" is in the Greek an infinitive used as an imperative, which was a military use.[38] The fallen warriors still use military language. They were used to receiving and giving orders, and so as they lie dead, having obeyed the orders given to them, so they in turn command the stranger who passes by and expect that their command will be obeyed. The pathos is complicated by the authoritarian tone.

A scrap of song by Praxilla of Sicyon has the dying Adonis say,

> Loveliest of what I leave behind is the sunlight,
> and loveliest after that the shining stars,
>   and the moon's face,
> but also cucumbers that are ripe, and pears,
> ·   and apples.[39]

The list of beloved things moves from the visual and sensual delight of the brightness and warmth and clarity of the sun to the purely visual pleasure of the paler reflection of that light in the moon and stars — appropriate for the coming of death as the light of life fades. But then, in a new and altogether unexpected burst of strength and memory, the immediate and fully sensual delights of fruits and vegetables are made equal to the distant starlight. Things close at hand that please the eye and hand and mouth and nose are as precious as the distant and noble lights of heaven. We learn again that simple things are not ordinary things.

In the Christian liturgy one finds examples of such brief songs that assume a great deal of familiarity with the resources of the tradition on the part of the congregation. In the Roman and in the Lutheran eucharistic rites a Verse may be sung by a cantor or choir immediately before the reading of the Gospel for the day to welcome and prepare for the reading by connecting it with a theme of the feast or the season. The principal characteristic of the Verse, except in Lent, is the Alleluia, the favorite and perpetual song of the church. During the Easter season St. Augustine preached about the meaning of that deeply significant word.

> Our thoughts in this present life should turn on the praise of God, because it is in praising God that we shall rejoice forever in the life to come; and none can be ready for the next life unless they train themselves for it now. . . .
>
> Because there are these two periods of time — the one that now is, beset with the trials and troubles of this life, and the other to come, a life of everlasting serenity and joy — we are given two liturgical seasons, one before Easter and the other after. The season before Easter signifies the troubles in which we live here and now, while the time after Easter, which we are celebrating at present, signifies that happiness that will be ours in the future. What we commemorate before Easter is what we experience in this life; what we celebrate after Easter points to something we do not yet possess. That is why we keep the first season with fasting and prayer; but now the fast is over and we devote the present season to praise. Such is the meaning of the *Alleluia* we sing. . . .
>
> Now therefore, brethren, we urge you to praise God. That is what we are telling each other when we say *Alleluia*. You say to your neighbor, "Praise the Lord!" and your neighbor says the same to you. We are all urging one another to praise the Lord, and all are thereby doing what each of us urges the other to do. But see that your praise comes from your whole being; in other words, see that you praise God not only with your lips and voices, but with your minds, your lives, and all your actions.[40]

Alleluia, the song of the resurrection faith, is sung to welcome the Gospel. To prepare for the proclamation of the Good News, words fail.

The word spoken breaks out into song, and song gives way to ecstatic syllables of joy, that greatest of all songs the human voice can sing, the song of the courts of heaven, Alleluia. The elaborate, ecstatic melismata sung to *Alleluia* was apparently a Christian innovation: "We know of no ancient pagan music in which a single syllable of text was extended by many notes of melody."[41] "Alleluia," that word rich with resonance, whenever it appears in the liturgy requires a melody. Merely to speak "alleluia" is to deprive it of life.

The (Alleluia) Verses that are sung in conjunction with the alleluia before the Gospel are usually extraordinarily concentrated and rich for those with ears to hear and the resources with which to respond to them with an "inner song." An example is the Verse for the First Sunday in Advent. It is in the translation in the *Lutheran Book of Worship* simply,

> Alleluia.
> . Show us your mercy, O Lord,
> and give us your salvation.
> Alleluia. (Ps. 85:7)

On the face of it, alone and spoken, that may sound rather flat and pedestrian, bland and predictable biblical language. But, especially when the Verse is sung, we are encouraged to respond to its suggestiveness. This plea for the dual graces of God's steadfast love and God's salvation takes Old Testament language and concepts and applies them to New Testament experience, joining then and now. We are the old Israel waiting for the fullness of God's promises. The traditional Gospel for the First Sunday in Advent, fortunately still an option in the Lutheran lectionary, is the story of Jesus' triumphal entry into Jerusalem with the cry of Zechariah ringing in our ears, "Behold your king comes to you!" Ancient prophecy, the longing of the ages, Jesus' lifetime, the experience of the church through the ages, and our own time are bound together. We at the beginning of the twenty-first century can still cry out with urgency and insistence, "Show us your mercy; give us your salvation." Singing can make that plea more urgent and compelling so that it becomes our song and our prayer also. Then the answer to our pleading is given as Jesus rides into his city in triumph and the Gospel fulfills the longing of the Verse, "Behold your king!" And that proclamation becomes a preparation for and announcement of our encounter with the coming king in proclamation and in sacrament until all is fulfilled in the kingdom of heaven.

In the *Lutheran Book of Worship* the Verse for the Sunday of the Passion ("Palm Sunday") is simply, "The hour has come for the Son of Man to be glorified." This Verse, from John 12:23, is sung to introduce the long Passion Gospel, two chapters of Matthew or Mark or Luke, and the paradoxical and revolutionary point is quietly yet thrillingly made that the Passion is Christ's glorification. This final struggle against darkness and death is his long-awaited "hour," the time of his triumph. He goes forth to die, a conqueror setting out in victory. With that understanding made clear, the congregation can hear aright the story of his suffering, death, and burial.

In the Lutheran rite, the Verse for Easter Day is in two parts. The first part, from Romans 6:9, is used at the beginning of each of the Verses for the Easter season.

> Alleluia.
>> Christ being raised from the dead
>> will die no more.
>> Death has no more dominion over him.

The use of this Verse throughout Easter binds the Fifty Days together and directs our attention to the victory of God that is celebrated throughout the "week of weeks." Death's power is broken, and eternal life is opened to all who live in Christ. The second part of the Verse for Easter Day is from Psalm 118:24:

>> This is the day which the Lord has made;
>> we will rejoice and be glad in it.
> Alleluia.

This day — that is, both Easter Day and its reflection every Sunday — is made holy by God's victory. The final Alleluia then breaks out even beyond itself to issue in the expansion of the Easter song in the sequence hymn, sung before the reading of the Gospel. The *Lutheran Book of Worship* directs that this hymn be "Christians, to the Paschal Victim" (no. 137), the *victimae paschali*, which may perhaps be sung by a single voice or, more dramatically, by two voices, a narrator and Mary Magdalene. Then the Gospel is read, especially the traditional Gospel, John 20:1–18, telling of the Magdalene's encounter with the risen Lord.

Another example of brief songs in the liturgy that assume familiarity
with the Bible and Christian tradition is found in the Offertory. These
proper (that is, variable) texts, tying together the offering by the congregation of its gifts of money and bread and wine and the offering of
the congregation of itself to the theme of the particular celebration of
the day or season, are somewhat longer than the Verses, but they too
require an inner song to respond to the suggestive allusions. As an example, consider the proper Offertory appointed in the *Lutheran Book of
Worship* for the feast of the Baptism of Our Lord, the First Sunday after
the Epiphany, from Psalm 29:2–4:

> Ascribe to the Lord the glory due his name;
>   worship the Lord in holy array.
> The voice of the Lord is upon the waters,
>   the Lord is upon the mighty waters.
> The voice of the Lord is powerful;
>   the voice of the Lord is full of majesty.

Old Testament verses are used to celebrate a New Testament event:
the mystical association of God and the waters goes all the way back to
the beginning of the creation account in the first chapter of Genesis,
and the ancient theme is made use of at the Epiphany. The majestic
voice of the Father blessing the Son is foreshadowed, "The voice of
the Lord is upon the waters"; the congregation's offering of the sacrifice of thanksgiving is invited, "Ascribe to the Lord the glory due his
name."

The Offertory for the First Sunday in Lent underscores the proper
understanding of the theme and the message of Lent: repentance. The
text is from Ezekiel 18:30–32:

> Repent and turn from your sins,
>   lest iniquity be your ruin.
> Cast away from you all the sins
>   which you have committed against me,
> and get yourselves a new heart
>   and a new spirit.
> For I have no pleasure in the death of anyone,
> says the Lord of hosts,
>   so turn to me and live.

This Offertory reminds the congregation that it is with such sacrifices (of the human heart and desire and will) that God, whose desire is for life, not punishment, is well pleased.

A third example of the value of the proper Offertory in unfolding the mystery of the Christian Gospel is that appointed for Pentecost, from Ephesians 5:5, 18–20:

> Look carefully, then, how you walk,
>   not as unwise but as wise;
> and be filled with the Spirit,
>   addressing one another in psalms and hymns
>   and spiritual songs,
> singing and making melody to the Lord
>   with all your heart,
> always and for everything giving thanks
> in the name of our Lord Jesus Christ
>   to God the Father.

Again, the sacrifice of thanksgiving is urged and the role of the Holy Spirit in inspiring songs of thanksgiving is acknowledged. When the church sings praise, it is the Spirit of God breathing and moving within it who prompts and shapes and fills the joyful songs.

Sometimes there is a deliberate echo of the Verse in the Offertory, tying these two propers together with a thread of continuity. Such a thread can be seen on the Feast of the Epiphany. The Verse is the familiar words of the Magi:

> Alleluia.
> We have seen his star in the East
> and have come to worship him.
> Alleluia.

The Gospel that follows tells their story. These mysterious and shadowy seers offered their gifts to the infant God in accordance with the ancient prophecy from Isaiah 60:1, recalled in the Offertory:

> Arise, shine, for your light has come,
>   and the glory of the Lord has risen upon you.
> They shall bring gold and frankincense,
>   and shall proclaim the praise of the Lord.
> We have seen his star in the East
>   and have come with gifts to worship the Lord.

Isaiah foretold the offering, the Magi exemplified and fulfilled the prophet's vision, and the congregation, offering its gifts, joins their worshipful generosity and continues the living line of the Gospel into the present time. Thus the singing of these suggestive texts deepens the devotion of those who take the time to consider them and enables the congregation to join more fervently in the Spirit-inspired and Spirit-filled songs and to sing at last the glorious and splendid song of heaven in the perpetual voice of the church, alleluia.

The concentrated richness of the complex event of text and melody and movement that the individual is invited to unlock and release is not only an ancient understanding and practice. In the final third of the twentieth century literary criticism developed an interest in the response of the reader to a work of literature.[42] A leading exponent of such an approach, Wolfgang Iser, has explained:

> The phenomenological theory of art lays full stress on the idea that, in considering a literary work, one must take into account not only the actual text but also, and in equal measure, the actions involved in responding to that text. . . . The work is more than the text, for the text only takes on life when it is realized, and furthermore the realization is by no means independent of the individual disposition of the reader — though this in turn is acted upon by the different patterns of the text. The convergence of text and reader brings the literary work into existence, and this convergence can never be precisely pinpointed, but must always remain virtual, as it is not to be identified either with the reality of the text or with the individual disposition of the reader.[43]

The reader uses the various perspectives offered by the text to relate the patterns to one another and so sets the work in motion, "and this very process results ultimately in the awakening of responses within himself. Thus reading causes the literary work to unfold its inherently dynamic character."[44] There is, therefore, the text created by the author (or in the case of modern liturgy, by the committee), and there is the realization of that text that is accomplished by the reader of the literary work or the users of the liturgical text; and always both text and reader-user function as a part of the interpretative community. Liturgical as well as literary texts can thus transform their use "into a creative process that is far above mere perception of what is written." The text "activates our own faculties, enabling us to recreate the world it presents" and produces a dimension that is not the text itself or the imagination of the reader but the coming together of the two.[45] Thus in both a literary work and a liturgy, the textual latency awaits actualization, and the richness of the actualization is complex and it is creative.[46] Using the liturgy, like reading, is incomplete unless it enters the consciousness of the participant, making an effect that must be ethical and returning as action to a world that is not yet perfect, waiting to be changed.[47]

Multiplicity of Meaning

Such a wealth of interaction is difficult to comprehend. To compound the difficulty, there is abroad a popular naive linguistic positivism that excludes or severely limits allusion, multivalence, ambiguity.

In the revision of hymn texts for inclusion in modern hymnals one finds abundant examples of "dumbing down" in the elimination of imagery, biblical allusion, troublesome phrases and stanzas that can be taken in more than one way. And, it may be noted, hymnals do not often agree as to what is in need of change. Compare, for example, the alterations to traditional hymn texts made in the hymnals of two closely related churches, the *Lutheran Book of Worship* (1978) and the Episcopal *Hymnal 1982* (actually published in 1985). Joseph Addison's familiar hymn sings,

> When all thy mercies, O my God,
>   My rising soul surveys,
> Transported with the view, I'm lost
>   In wonder, love, and praise....
>
> Through every period of my life
>   Thy goodness I'll pursue,
> And after death, in distant worlds,
>   The glorious theme renew.

The *Lutheran Book of Worship* has changed "thy" to "your" (as one might expect), "rising" to "waking" (thereby losing the sense of elevation included in the original), and "through every period of my life" to "through every passing phase of life" apparently to prevent some from hearing *menses* in the word "period" (but if some hear that, is it so utterly inappropriate?). And there is a whiff of condescension in "phase," the voice of a harried parent who knows (or hopes) that the present

difficulty with a child will soon pass. The *Hymnal 1982*, like its predecessor, did not include the stanza "Through every period of my life" and
makes only one change in the hymn; it occurs in the stanza

> O how shall words with equal warmth
> The gratitude declare
> That glows within my ravished heart?
> But thou canst read it there.

"Ravished" is replaced by "fervent." The alteration of that one word
makes a considerable shift from the human heart as the object of divine assault to the heart as the locus of fervor. The emphasis has been
shifted from the action of God, violent though it is, to the condition
of the heart. (Replacing "ravished" — that is, "raped" — with "captive"
or "captured" would have retained the emphasis on God's action.) The
discomforting imagery of the exercise of dominating power in violent
assault with clear sexual overtones was no doubt too strong for modern
sensitivities, but it did echo a strain of powerful imagery in such devotional writers as Teresa of Avila and John Donne, who at the conclusion
of his Holy Sonnet xiv has the speaker exclaim,

> Take me to You, imprison me, for I
> Except You enthrall me, never shall be free,
> Nor ever chaste, except You ravish me.

(It is worth bearing in mind that in traditional devotional practice, the
soul, whether of a male or a female, is always portrayed as a female.)

There is, E. B. White reminds us, no average reader, "capable of
reading only what tests Easy," and to contend that the writer should aim
at or below this level is a presumptuous and degrading idea. Writing,
he says, is an act of faith, not a trick of grammar, and a writer who
questions the capacity of the person at the other end of the line and
writes at a level calculated to be easily understood by such a reader "is
not a writer at all, merely a schemer."[48]

Stephen Prickett has offered an illuminating analysis of the passage
in 1 Kings 19:8–12, which tells of Elijah's meeting with God on Mount
Horeb. He illustrates from the Good News Bible, the New English Bible,
and the Jerusalem Bible how the modern translators "seem to be quite
unanimous in *rejecting* any ambiguity or oddity in the original."[49] One of
the translators of the New English Bible, Kenneth Grayston, is quoted
as boasting that, "in equivocal passages, the translators had to come

off the fence and say 'we think it means this.' In ambiguous passages we had to write out the meaning plainly, and in obscure passages, to refrain from reproducing nonsense in translation."[50] The translators, sweeping away the literal sense, attempted to make clear all ambiguity, for that approach is judged "more culturally acceptable to modern sensibilities."[51] C. H. Sisson comments on this approach, "The tension between the relatively remote text and contemporary speech has gone; the possibility of extracting from the original anything which has the air of novelty to current ignorance is precluded."[52] In Prickett's view, the entire passage in 1 Kings 19 is "enigmatic and puzzling" once one begins looking at it. What was the fire? An electric storm? A bush fire? Was it connected with the earthquake? What did it burn? What is the status of the third-person narrator? Is it Elijah himself? Prickett focuses on the "still small voice" of the Authorized Version, which he describes as "a remarkably accurate translation," with "an obscurity and ambiguity that is at least faithful to the original."[53] He suggests that the Hebrew *kol dammanah dakkah* may be translated "a voice of thin silence" (recalling that in Elizabethan English "small" could still mean "thin"), but the modern versions "produce an implicitly naturalistic reading rather than follow the mysteriously suggestive Hebrew." The Good News Bible has "the soft whisper of a voice"; the New English Bible has "a low murmuring sound"; the Jerusalem Bible "the sound of a gentle breeze."[54]

Part of what separates modern English from its past is an intolerance of ambiguity. John Bois, a translator and member of the final revision committee for part of the Authorized Version of the New Testament, indicated that he and his committee were careful to preserve textual ambiguity. "We have not thought that the indefinite sense ought to be defined."[55] Modern users of English expect narrative to make clear whether it is to be taken as "fact" or "fiction," and we are uneasy when the two genres are mixed.

> We need to know whether Elijah's theophany was visionary or miraculous — whether the "voice" is to be understood as "internal," an event presumed to be *within* Elijah's own mind, or "external," producing a phenomenon in nature to be detected by the presence of a witness.[56]

The New English Bible, with its "low murmuring sound" (the Revised English Bible has "a faint murmuring sound"), has decided that the phenomenon was natural. Prickett observes that not one of the three modern translations he examines "manages to suggest an inherent peculiarity about the event that might indicate a quite *new* kind of experience. Indeed, it is precisely the oddity or paradox in the original text that the modern translators... found either untranslatable, or, more probably, unacceptable."[57] We can be "modern," apparently, only by dealing with the whole story on only one level: it must be either miraculous *or* natural. Such rationalism seems to strike at the heart of the original story.

Ambiguity is characteristic of more than the religious dimensions of experience; it is inherent in humanity itself. "Contradiction is the very element of human existence," Ernst Cassirer observed.[58]

The apprehension and expression of delight in the richness of creation requires a language that is appropriately rich and multi-dimensioned. Such language must be capable of suggesting to its hearers new connections and fresh conjunctions, bearing at once both pleasure and instruction. What Northrop Frye says of the Bible might also be said of the liturgy (and of the world as well):

> It... includes an immense variety of material, and the unifying forces that hold it together cannot be the rigid forces of doctrinal consistency or logic, which soon would collapse under cultural stress, but the more flexible ones of imaginative unity, which is founded on metaphor. Metaphor... is an identity of various things, not the sham uniformity in which all details are alike.[59]

Such a view presupposes a certain sophistication. Much of education teaches us to be precise. As essential and worthwhile as such training is, it can nonetheless pose problems if it cuts us off from the ability to hold varying ideas and insights at once. A single-minded pursuit of clarity and precision does not easily tolerate ambiguity. If two or more interpretations of an action are possible, a scientific and rationalistic culture may demand a decision about which one of the several ideas is correct. There is a bias toward simplicity in all learning, but even with regard to natural science Alfred North Whitehead warned,

> The aim of science is to seek the simplest explanation of complex facts. We are apt to fall into the error of thinking that the facts are simple because simplicity is the goal of our quest. The guiding motto in the life of every natural philosopher should be, "Seek simplicity and distrust it."[60]

Exclusive precision is not helpful in many significant areas of our experience. G. K. Chesterton notes that the ordinary person has permitted the twilight.

> He always cared more for truth than for consistency. If he saw two truths that seemed to contradict each other, he would take the two truths and the contradiction along with them. His spiritual sight is stereoscopic, like his physical sight: he sees two different pictures at once and yet sees all the better for that.[61]

The insight is present in English poetry also. What Richard H. Fogle has said of John Keats's "Ode to a Nightingale" is also true of Keats's other great odes:

> they express an exquisite awareness of the existence of joy and melancholy, pleasure and pain, and art and life. They express a feeling that these are inseparable, although not identical, and they express acceptance of the inseparability of the elements of human experience.[62]

Mircea Eliade has observed that "the symbol, the myth, and the image are of the very substance of the spiritual life."[63]

> Symbolic thinking is not the exclusive privilege of the child, of the poet, or of the unbalanced mind: it is consubstantial with human existence, it comes before language and discursive reason. The symbol reveals certain aspects of reality — the deepest aspects — which defy other means of knowledge.[64]

Greek mythology, in joining Hephaestos and Aphrodite as husband and wife, the ugly and lame smith with the perfection of physical beauty, has exhibited a mature and profound awareness of the complexity of reality. Eliade has written of classical Greek religion,

> Like the Greek people itself, its gods are the result of a grandiose synthesis. It is by virtue of this long process of confrontation, symbiosis, coalescence, and synthesis that the Greek divine forces were able to reveal all their virtualities.[65]

As a specific example, he observes of the Greek goddess Artemis,

> Under her many and sometimes contradictory aspects we divine the plurality of the archaic divine forms revalorized and integrated

into a vast structure by the Greek religious genius. . . . She has always retained a paradoxical character, illustrated, above all, by the coexistence of contradictory themes (e.g. virginity-maternity). The creative imagination of the Greek poets, mythographers, and theologians divined that such a coexistence of contraries can suggest one of the mysteries of divinity.[66]

Such mystery is of course not limited to Greek mythology. It is present elsewhere as well, notably in Egyptian mythology and religion that actively sought out varied explanations, myths, and stories in order to portray the diversity of experience. Christianity too has treasured the conjunction of contraries. St. Peter Chrysologos, for example, preached on the Feast of the Epiphany,

> Today the Magi find, crying in a manger, the one they have followed as he shone in the sky. Today the Magi see clearly, in swaddling clothes, the one they have long awaited as he lay hidden among the stars.

> Today the Magi gaze in deep wonder at what they see: heaven on earth, earth in heaven, man in God, God in man, one whom the whole universe cannot contain now enclosed in a tiny body.[67]

Most highly treasured of all contraries, of course, is the *Theotokos*, the God-bearer, the mortal woman who is the mother of God, the virgin mother and her Son, the God-man, who by dying put death to death.

A distinctive characteristic of both biblical and liturgical language is that the central images exist at once on several levels. A useful way of uncovering the various layers and dimensions of meaning is the practice of allegory. Ineptly handled, the allegorical method can become too neat, a restricting order imposed by an authoritarian interpreter on the richness of the symbols of Scripture and religion, taming and impoverishing them.[68] Sometimes that allegorical approach could leave the plain literal meaning of the text far behind in flights of intellectual and imaginative exercise. That happened in medieval interpretations of liturgy that found allegorical meaning in every action.[69] The priest's moving from the Epistle side of the altar to the Gospel side was said to represent Jesus' journey from Pilate to Herod; the Lavabo represented Pilate washing his hands. At its best, however, the allegorical approach inspired multiple interpretations and emphasized ambiguities.

For allegory is not merely an extended metaphor, seeing one thing in terms of another, portraying abstract qualities in tangible representations. It is the capacity to see a situation simultaneously under different aspects, each existing on its own level, in its own right, yet at the same time forming a part of a greater order in relation to which its complete meaning is to be understood. The convergence of attributes upon a single point enriches our understanding by conferring upon it a spiritual significance without detracting from the concreteness of the original conception.[70]

Allegory may be dealt with in one of two ways: tightly, neatly, leaving no loose ends, giving a kind of satisfaction; or it can be dealt with loosely, suggestively, in a way that stimulates the imagination more than it satisfies the intellect.[71] For example, the fifteenth-century morality play *Everyman* employs allegory in a neat or tight way; the characters bear names like "Goods," "Five-wits," "Kindred," to say nothing of the principal character who gives his name to the play. In such a work as the fourteenth-century *Piers Plowman,* on the other hand, the greatest of all the alliterative poems of social protest, allegory is handled more loosely, sparking the imagination of the writer and the reader alike and frustrating those who would summarize the poem.[72]

Interpreters of the Bible have from the first insisted on the multiplicity of senses of interpretation, for "Scripture, like the visible world, is a great mirror reflecting God, and therefore all and every kind of truth."[73] God's will and words were thus hidden in Scripture, which, like a medieval cathedral, spoke to people in a language of symbols.[74] In the development of the interpretation of Holy Scripture, as Umberto Eco understands it, the "symbolic mode" of early tradition, a loose form of allegory, inspired multiple interpretations and emphasized ambiguities. In time, however, this was replaced by an "allegorical code," a far tighter, neater use of allegory, imposed by an increasingly authoritarian church. Order was imposed on the richness by taming and impoverishing it.[75] Some degree of order is necessary, to be sure, to permit interpretation of the chaotic reality of Scripture and of human experience in general, but meaning is best described not with simplified structures but with the encyclopedic experience of the hearer or observer. The interpretation of metaphors is especially torturous and depends on a rich shared cultural framework. What is always to be avoided is the ready-made approach that cuts reality down to size to control it. The labyrinths of language can be described and understood

but not at the cost of curtailing its meanderings.[76] The chaos needs to
be ordered without reduction, oversimplification, and loss.

From the time of John Cassian (died ca. 435)[77] and Augustine
through the Middle Ages,[78] a system of allegorization was developed
according to which ultimately four meanings were to be sought in every
text: the literal (what happened), the allegorical (what to believe), the
tropological or moral (what to do), and the anagogical or spiritual
(what to hope). Cassian provided what has become a classic example of such exegetical depth, "Jerusalem" in Galatians 4:22ff. Literally
and historically Jerusalem is the city in Judaea; allegorically it represents the church, the city of God; tropologically or morally it represents
the human soul; anagogically or spiritually it points to the heavenly city.
The symbols of the liturgy often function in the same way and are to
be understood on several levels at once. At its best such an interpretative approach can keep the text rooted in reality so that people can see
the past in terms of their own experiences and, yet more profoundly,
see their experiences in terms of the communal memory of the great
formative events of the past. The biblical story is uncovered, and one
discovers oneself as a participant in it.[79] Zion, a favorite title for Lutheran churches, is geographically a hill; it is by extension the city built
on the hill; then the dwelling of God, both heavenly and earthly; then
the hope of restoration; then the transhistorical goal of the Christian
pilgrimage, our ultimate and abiding home. The European settlers of
New England saw themselves as the descendents of Israel, reliving its
experience in the wilderness.[80] The Exodus was understood to be happening again with the settling of North America, and the archetypal
biblical story was extended into their present and they became participants in it. The Exodus may be understood to happen again any
time oppressed people struggle for freedom: a present struggle for liber-
ation has meaning when seen as having roots in the Exodus, the great
and archetypal deliverance from slavery to freedom in all the profound
richness of those words.

Like the language of the Bible, liturgical symbols, when they are
alive, never lose their concreteness, their roots in human experience —
a letter, a bath, a meal. Such concrete historical rooting is essential, if
for no other reason than to command continuing attention. As Wallace
Stevens observed, "Eventually an imaginary world is entirely without
interest"[81] and again "What is divinity if it can come / Only in silent
shadows and dreams?"[82]

Yet there is a useful playfulness in the allegorical language of the liturgy. Allegory, saying one thing and meaning another, is an indication of the nature of language itself, "constantly telling us that something is what it is not."[83] It is therefore a valuable technique in attempting to represent the world while remaining alert to its ambiguities. Allegory

> exhibits something of the perpetually fluctuating, uncertain status of the world it depicts. Such a figurative world, as Plato argued, is not susceptible to a definitive treatment, but only to provisional description — to an *eikos mythos,* a likely story.... At the same time, such an account may at least suggest something of the value of its subject. For allegory, which is always pointing toward a goal that lies beyond it, is forever having to come to terms with its own provisionality. In the process, it encourages its readers not only to aspire toward some world of perfect fulfillment, but to direct attention to the limited world of which they are a part.[84]

By continuing to subvert itself, allegory is a useful reminder of the provisional nature of our attempts to depict a fugitive world.

One must give attention to the rhythm of the liturgy, the move-ment up and down, rapid and slower, exalted and somber, penitential and joyful. A narrow focus on the words of the text of the liturgy may neglect a larger way of responding to its richness that was available to past centuries in which large and controlling images form in the mind as the text unfolds and determine the way in which it is received and remembered.

Many medieval writers, for instance, speak not only of reading or hearing a poem but also of "seeing" it. "When one hears a tale read," declared Richard de Fournivall, "one perceives the wondrous deeds as if one were to see them taking place."[85] Because of its power of visualiza-tion, the imagination was sometimes described as the "eye" of the mind. In fact, imaginative insight was only one of several kinds of mental vision that were distinguished in late medieval thought. Peter of Limo-ges in *De Oculo Morali* described the process of moral perception in terms of movement from the carnal eye of sense to the interior eye of imagination, to the mind's eye of reason, and finally to the heart's eye of the will.[86] According to the theory of "anagogic" or "uplifting" im-agery found in *The Celestial Hierarchies* (Pseudo-Dionysus?), Scripture employs poetic and imaginative representations of sacred things out of deference to our limited human understanding. The mind is supposed to proceed from the sensible to the intelligible, from sacred imagery to those spiritual realities that lie beyond figure and type.

Allegory then teaches us that things are not necessarily what they seem; they may be richer, deeper, grander, more treacherous than may be apparent. It also suggests that truth is not something that we already possess but is perhaps best understood as a goal toward which we move and which draws us on. "The light which we have gained," wrote John Milton in *Areopagitica* (1644), "was given us, not to be ever staring on, but by it to discover onward things more remote from our knowledge."[87] If truth is in any sense already our possession, it is something that we may have but do not yet fully apprehend or understand. Symbols, together with symbolic language, tease and entice and urge us along the way toward understanding.

Chapter Four

MUSIC:
TRANSCENDENT LANGUAGE

A s has already been noticed, it is an impoverishment to limit liturgical language to words or to a text. When it is alive, liturgical language is always accompanied and supported by music. Moreover, for most of Christianity, especially Orthodoxy and Lutheranism, liturgy, in addition to words, always and almost necessarily involves music.[1] The entirely said or spoken service is nearly unknown in these two communions. The Roman Catholic Church for centuries had its "low mass," spoken, not sung; the Anglican Church has its 8 A.M. Holy Communion, which is very often a said service. But Lutherans expect hymns, without which a service to them seems barren and unsatisfying, and they also expect chant, a service that is sung at least by the congregation even if the presiding minister cannot or will not sing the leader's part. And when family devotions used to be common among Lutherans the singing of hymns was a regular feature of such worship in the home.

In all the world there has apparently never been a civilization without song. "No songless people has ever been discovered," declares the *Oxford Companion to Music.*[2] C. M. Bowra in his study *Primitive Song* found only a single South American tribe not possessing song in our usual meaning of the word. Elsewhere, with this one possible exception, in all the ancient societies that we know anything about, there has been a profound regard for music and specifically for song and a deep understanding of its power.

In *The Burning Fountain* Philip Wheelwright tells the Estonian legend of how the god of song Wannemunne once descended onto the Domberg and there in a sacred wood invited all creatures to listen to music of divine beauty. Each creature learned some fragment of the music. The forest learned its rustling, the stream its roar, the wind the shrillest tones, the birds the prelude to the song. The fish lifted their eyes out of the water but their ears remained below the surface, and so, although they saw and imitated the movements of the god's mouth, they remained dumb. Only humanity grasped it all, and therefore human song pierces the depths of the heart and ascends into the dwellings of the gods. Humanity alone of all creation knows the full power of song.[3]

> To listen for the voice of Wisdom, or the Muse, or Wannemunne, or Conscience, or Christ, means standing ready to be guided by an imperative not wholly of one's own making, yet to which one's psyche responds at a level of depth. It is an apprenticeship in singing the full song.[4]

Indeed, recalling the opening chapters of Luke's Gospel with the songs of Zechariah, Mary, the angels, and Simeon, it may be said that the Christian church was born in song.[5]

Songs of Power

Athanasius declared in a letter to Marcellinus that the desire of the soul is to be beautifully disposed and this is achieved by singing praise. "In this way that which is disturbing and rough and disorderly in it is smoothed away, and that which causes grief is healed when we sing psalms."[6] Throughout the ancient world songs are honored as creative and healing and transforming powers. To take just one diverse culture, that of the Native Americans, as an example, one finds that "in nearly every Indian myth the creator SINGS things into life."[7] The sung word is creative, for song enhances the power of the spoken word. There is a Papago "Song to Pull Down the Clouds":

> At the edge of the world
> It is growing light.
> Up rears the light.
> Just yonder the day dawns,
> Spreading over the night.[8]

The title reveals that the song is not just a description of the dawn of a new day. The song actually participates in the action of renewal, assisting in pulling down the obscuring clouds so that the light can spread

over the night. By this song the singer helps the morning come. There
is this Papago song to heal the earth:

> Now as the night is over us
>> we are singing the songs that were given to us.
> You see the clouds beginning to form on top of the mountains.
> They look like little white feathers.
> You will see them shake like feathers in a wind.
> Soon the raindrops will fall and make our country beautiful.[9]

The song received from the ancestors is more than an observation or a
prediction; it is a participation in the healing process, for its words help
to bring the renewing rain. There is this healing and transforming song
of the Ojibwa (Chippewa):

> You are a spirit.
> I am making you a spirit.
> In the place where I sit
> I am making you a spirit.[10]

The little song is not only an expression of sympathy for and solidar-
ity with the dying person. It is itself a participation in the process of
transformation. The song helps make the dying person a spirit, and the
singer who simply sits and sings is awed by the power of the song that
reaches "from the place where I sit" into the next world. There is this
little burst of triumphant power as a Chippewa singer exults in song:

> My music
> reaches
> to the sky.[11]

We listen to the pride of the singer whose music flies beyond the earth
and who is intoxicated by the soaring power of song. It is not merely a
general praise of the wonder of music but a personal triumph also: "My
music." The singer has a share in this transcendent power. The music
flies as far as music can reach, and the little song joins the two worlds,
the home of the gods and the earth. The gulf is spanned not by a visible bridge but by the unseen and intangible power of song. The song
becomes a means by which the gods and humans can communicate. It
is a poem of the exultant pride of a singer who rejoices in an enormous
gift; yet there is a hint of limitation here too, for the song may perhaps
not penetrate the heavens after all.

Ruth Underhill summarized the role of Native American music:

> Song was not simply self-expression. It was a magic which called
> upon the powers of Nature and constrained them to man's will.
> People sang in trouble, in danger, to cure the sick, to confound
> their enemies, and to make the crops grow.[12]

Singing participated in and exerted power.

Humanity has intuitively sensed that something connects all creation, embracing its contradictions without being destroyed by them,
harmonizing differences. That something is as elemental and pervasive as music.[13] In Pythagorean astronomy the spheres, hollow globes
or orbs in which the heavenly bodies were set, revolved about the earth
as a common center, giving forth sounds inaudible to human ears.[14]
Pythagoras, having ascertained that the pitch of notes depends on the
rapidity of vibrations and also that the planets move at different rates of
motion, concluded that the planets must make sounds proportionate to
their different rates, which rise with distance from the earth; and that,
as all things in nature are harmoniously made, the different sounds must
harmonize as "the music of the spheres," which we never hear because
we hear it all the time. The harmony of the universe was a remarkably
persistent idea. Variations of the concept are found throughout classical times and in Dante, Shakespeare, and Milton, and even in certain
popular hymns such as "This Is My Father's World." John Dryden in his
"Song for St. Cecelia's Day" (1687), given memorable energy by Han-
del's fine score (1739), described the creative and organizing work of
harmony:

> From harmony, from heav'nly harmony
>   This universal frame began:
>   From harmony to harmony
> Thro' all the compass of the notes it ran,
> The diapason closing full in Man.
>   •
>
> As from the power of sacred lays
>   The spheres began to move,
> And sung the great Creator's praise
>   To all the bless'd above;
> So, when the last and dreadful hour
> This crumbling pageant shall devour,

> The trumpet shall be heard on high,
> The dead shall live, the living die,
> And Musick shall untune the sky.

Early Christians found in Christ such a melody of harmonious organization, the music of the cosmos, and found in such psalm verses as 33:3, referring to a "new song," a foreshadowing of the songs of Christianity occasioned by the coming of Christ, himself the New Song. Clement of Alexandria (ca. 150–ca. 215) is the earliest witness to offer an extensive statement of this idea. He explains that the first letter of Jesus' name, *iota*, which signifies ten, is implied in the "ten-stringed instrument" of Psalm 33:2, which reveals "Jesus, the Word, manifested in the element of the decad."[15] Clement begins his *Protrepticus* (*Protreptikos*) or *Exhortation* with a greatly extended metaphor declaring that the musical mythology of ancient Greece has been superseded by the New Song, who is Christ the Logos, "the song which is called new, although most ancient."[16] The New Song establishes order, harmony, and concord. It ordered the universe and tuned the discord of the elements in one harmonious arrangement. "This pure song, the stay of the universe and the harmony of all things," freed the sea and set its boundaries, tamed fire, ordered "this great world" as well as the little world of humankind, opened the eyes of the blind, unstopped the ears of the deaf, reconciled disobedient humanity to God. The Word of God, the descendent yet predecessor of David, scorned lyre and cithara as lifeless instruments and sang instead on the many-voiced instrument of his bodily life to God and to humanity, itself an instrument. The Lord made humanity a beautiful breathing instrument after his own image, God's harp by reason of the music, God's pipe by reason of the breath of the Spirit, God's temple by reason of the Word, so that the music should resound, the Spirit inspire, and the temple receive its Lord. "This is the New Song, the shining manifestation among us now of the Word, who was in the beginning and before the beginning."[17]

The early church was uncomfortable with the use of song because of its association with pagan worship. Clement of Alexandria, quoting from Psalm 150, proposes the use of allegorical rather than actual musical instruments. Praise God with trumpet sound for he will raise the dead with the sound of the trumpet; praise God on the psaltery for the tongue is the psaltery of the Lord; praise God on the cithara, which is the mouth, played by the Spirit "as if by a plectum"; praise God with tympanum as the church meditates on "the resurrection of the flesh in the resounding membrane"; praise God on strings and the instrument, that is our body and its sinews "from which it derives its harmonious tension, and when strummed by the Spirit it gives off human notes"; praise God with clashing cymbals of the mouth; "Let everything that breathes praise the Lord" because God "watches over every breathing thing he has made."[18] John Chrysostom, commenting on Psalm 41:2, also makes instruments an allegory for the individual Christian.

> Here there is no need of... any sort of instrument; but if you wish, make of yourself a cithara, by mortifying the limbs of flesh and creating full harmony between body and soul. For when the flesh does not lust against the spirit, but yields to its commands, and perseveres along the path that is noble and admirable, you thus produce a spiritual melody.[19]

Likewise Jerome, accepting the Pauline injunction to use "psalms, hymns, and spiritual songs," (Eph. 5:18–20; Col. 3:16–17) notes that the melody is to be made "in your hearts." "We ought therefore to sing, to make melody, and to praise the Lord more with spirit than the voice."[20]

Heightened Speech

Art is no mere decoration added to give evidence of culture, a picture to hang on the wall to complete the decor, "something large and blue to complement the sofa fabric." Art is communication at its most intense. Poetry, as was shown in the preceding chapter, is elevated, intensified language. Ancient people knew this better than we do. Johan Huizinga in his provocative book *Homo Ludens: A Study of the Play Element in Culture* reminds us that

> Civilization is always slow to abandon the verse form as the chief means of expressing things of importance to the life of the community. Poetry everywhere precedes prose; for the utterance of solemn or holy things it is the only adequate vessel.[21]

So we find not only hymns but lengthy treatises like the Hindu *sutras* and *sastras* written in poetry as well as the early products of Greek philosophy and Empedocles and Lucretius. For Huizinga, it is not simply that verse was easier to memorize than prose but that poetry echoed the metrical and strophic structure of archaic society. Traces of poetry can be found in that most unlikely of places, the law. He notes that until 1868 the Japanese used to compose the weightiest parts of state documents in poetry, and he gives the powerful passage in Old Frisian law where the clause concerning the various "needs" or needful occasions on which an orphan's inheritance has to be sold suddenly breaks into lyrical form:

> The second need is when the year becomes dear and hot hunger passes over the land and the child is like to die of hunger. Then the mother must offer the child's patrimony for sale and buy their child cow and corn, etc. The third need is when the child is stark naked and houseless and dark fog comes and cold winter, and every man withdraws into house and home and warm hollows, and the wild beast seeks the hollow tree and the lee of the mountain where he may save his life. Then the unfledged child will weep and wail and lament his naked limbs and his want of shelter and his father who should have fostered him against hunger and the chill mists of winter, and who now lies dark and deep with four nails close covered under oak and earth.

Huizinga comments, "It seems to me that we are dealing here not so much with deliberate ornamentation as with the circumstance that the formulation of law still lay in that exalted sphere of the mind where poetic wording was the natural means of expression."[22] When the language of everyday communication — running the household, buying groceries, ordering furniture, gossiping about the neighbors — turns to more important matters — declaring love, forming thoughts about life and aging and death — it breaks its bonds to the commonplace and rises into poetry.

When language turns to the most important subject of all, worship, it breaks out into poetic expression and the poetry draws upon its ancient roots and emerges in song. Joseph Gelineau has observed,

> The word which is merely spoken is a somewhat incomplete form of human language. It suffices for ordinary utilitarian communications. But as soon as the word becomes charged with emotion, as soon as it is filled with power, as soon as it tends to identify itself with the content of its message — when, in fine, it has to signify

the sacredness of actions being performed — then it calls imperatively for number and melos, that is, for a musical form.... The complete word, the fully developed word, the sacred word, has the nature of song.[23]

Song arises "when oral speech no longer suffices."[24]

The roots of song are so deep that many have suggested that human beings could sing before they learned to talk[25] and that human language began as a kind of chant.[26] Song, it seems, was there from the beginning of civilization; it is as ancient as humanity itself. "Indeed, song is probably the mother not only of music and verse, but also of speech itself."[27] If this is in fact so, the language of the liturgy is not only a breaking out through successive layers of confinement as language ascends toward its grand subject; it is a return to the earliest experience of the race and is therefore a deeply powerful communication. Music releases a power, giving wings to the word. A Chinese lyric laments,

> No monk lives at the old temple, the Buddha has
>   toppled to the floor;
> One bell hangs high, bright with the evening sun.
> Sad that when only a tap is needed, no one now dares
> To rouse the notes of solemn music
>   that cram its ancient frame.[28]

The world is filled with latent sound waiting to be stirred and set free.

In song the potentialities of the power of words are revealed and released. C. M. Bowra observes that once words have begun to be accommodated to music, "they display qualities which might not be expected of them in their ordinary duties, and have not only lilt and balance but tone and quality."

> Primitive song is aware of this, and though it has tunes which complete and amplify its words, the words also are carefully fashioned for their own rhythm and self-contained, satisfying harmonies. They are more carefully chosen than other words and have the compelling power which comes when words are loaded with evocative meaning and enabled to make the most of this by their own distinction. The prime discovery of primitive song is that words are able to do this and in doing it add a new dimension to their use.[29]

Moreover, words by their sound and rhythm and sense can exert such a powerful hold on us that we can think of nothing else and so we speak of their power to enchant. This was not always a metaphor and is a reminder of what song once was and indeed what song still can be. The primal singer, like the Hebrew prophets, feels within "an eruptive, domineering force" which must be released upon others. The singer wishes to exert an influence, to impose a special vision, to create in others a state of mind that is more than understanding or sympathy and implies some sort of subordination to the singer's will.[30] In 2 Kings 3:15 we read, "Elisha said, 'Bring me a minstrel.' And when the minstrel played, the power of the Lord came upon him." Here again, music is used to evoke a trance out of which the prophet could give his oracle. Song is a participation in the divine force and power that are at work in the world, that take hold of a person and will not let go.

Because of this powerful, domineering energy that erupts into song, we naturally expect liturgical texts to involve song. But listen also to the sermons of non-liturgical African-American preachers and many Pentecostals. These preachers whose sermons must bear much of the burden of worship move, as the emotion builds, from mere prose into a sing-song punctuated with a kind of humming, a clear rhythm that captivates the congregation in its driving energy and musical cadence. It is a kind of Protestant chant. Jonathan Edwards, the staunch Calvinist, in a remarkable passage in his *Personal Narrative* reports how as a boy he was so overwhelmed by the beauty of nature that he could not refrain from breaking out into a chanting of the praise of the Creator.[31]

Poetry has its roots in music, and Ezra Pound noted that poetry to remain poetry never entirely loses that ancient connection and never moves too far from its source. "Poetry withers and dries out when it leaves music, or at least imagined music, too far behind it. Poets who are not interested in music are, or become, bad poets."[32]

Music is not only an ancient feature of language but a universal human phenomenon that may be bred into us from the womb.[33] Mothers while they are pregnant sing, and when they sing to their infants after they are born separation is suspended. "The mother having entered into her song, the child enters it too, they are fully together, anxiety is irrelevant, and sleep is easy."[34] Deeper than words, deeper than the individual is the impulse to song. Words are incomplete without melody, and without song each of us is incomplete also.

Anciently people knew that important words required melody and also that the resulting song required movement. Singing was usually accompanied by some kind of action such as a dance to emphasize or illustrate or punctuate the singing. "Words, music, and movement present a single unity and each element can be judged at its full worth only when it is at work with the others."[35] Thus, when we look at a liturgy, we cannot examine only the text any more than we can satisfactorily examine only the text of a Bach cantata. We must look at the words, to be sure, but we must also look at the music to which the words are set and examine the interplay between them. Even then we have not yet done enough, for we must also examine the movements that the text and the melodies require or suggest or inspire. What do the ministers and the congregation *do* before, during, after these texts are sung? Only by answering such questions can we have a comprehensive and satisfactory analysis of the liturgy.

Lessons of Music

These reflections on the importance of song in religious worship suggest several things that song can teach us about ourselves and about Christianity itself.

1. First of all, song is given, and then it is gone.[36] Each rendition is a unique and ephemeral experience (setting aside the matter of recordings and videotapes). A song may be sung over and over, week after week, year after year, but each rendering is really unrepeatable, for no two renderings are ever precisely the same. Each is a rare and precious experience because it cannot happen exactly that way again. (Sometimes that may be just as well, of course, but the uniqueness abides nonetheless.)

Each individual is the product of an unrepeatable conjunction of events. Each is a unique, unreproducible individual: there has never been, we suppose, nor can there ever be again anyone exactly like us in all the universe. We can never again find ourselves in exactly the same circumstances as we do this day. Songs and individuals are unique, and when they come together in a service of worship, that liturgical performance is unrepeatable, for never again will that same gathering of individuals with those particular situations and concerns and joys be possible. Similar gatherings may surely again take place, even week after week with the same congregation, but never can the same gathering occur again.

2. A song has a forward-driving energy. Neither the singer nor the hearer can linger or hesitate. Once begun, a song must be continued to the end.[37] When one reads a text, a poem for example, one is free to pause to reflect on a well-crafted or a puzzling passage. One is free to go back and reread a word or a line that was not clear or that was particularly interesting or pleasing. But that cannot happen with a song. The experience is continuous, progressive, and over it we have no control. We must submit to its energy and go with its movement. Otherwise we lose the creativity inherent in the performance. "Words are reinforced, blurred, belied, inspired to new meaning in a continual interplay."[38]

So it is, of course, with each life. There are passages we would like to skip over, and there are places where we would like to linger or repeat, but it cannot be. We must savor the good times while they last and endure the painful times until they pass. It is also true of the liturgy. Once a service of worship begins it continues until it is completed with that same forward-driving energy that is characteristic of song and of life as well. Indeed, in the Roman Catholic Church canon law requires that once a mass has begun it must be completed. The song, each life, each liturgy cannot be interrupted. Once begun, each must be continued to the end.

3. Music and specifically song give access to other dimensions of reality in addition to those dimensions of space and time where we find ourselves and other people and things separate and sequential.

> Because music exists, the tangible and visible cannot be the whole of the given world. The intangible and invisible is itself a part of this world, something to which we respond.[39]

Music, Victor Zuckerkandl contends, provides the shortest and least arduous, "perhaps even the most natural solvent of artificial boundaries between the self and others."[40] People sing in order to make sure, through direct experience, of their existence in a layer of reality where distinction and separation give way to unity.[41] The world to which music admits us is beyond that of space and time. We know it in harmony, "where two or more plainly distinct notes exist apart but simultaneous."[42] Harmony thus teaches a model of the unity of the church in which what is separate exists simultaneously with others and which together contribute to the existence and power and beauty of the whole. We know the world of musical experience also in the fact of tune, "when tones move around somewhere and come back to rest in some invisible place."[43] Tune may thus suggest the pilgrim character of the Christian life, a pilgrimage taking place in this world of space and time but somehow also above and beyond it, moving through space and time to find the promised rest in the place prepared for us by God:

> There is one further stage in this annihilation of distance in song: if we come into real unity with things sung about, those things cannot be separate in that dimension of reality from each other, either: "In the layer of reality whence the tones come and toward which they lead, not only the antithesis of 'I' and 'it' but also the distinctions between things are transcended. There must be a layer in which all things have their roots."[44]

The place to which music and song admit us, Zuckerkandl insists, is a place of unity, of communion of the self with all else that is. Song annihilates distance and time, joining present experience with past experiences. Past and present are experienced simultaneously.

Ritual does that also, transcending the divisions we know in time and space. In the Easter Vigil, most memorably, each church becomes the site of the tomb outside Jerusalem, and the troubling experience of the resurrection happens anew. The deacon sings the Exsultet, that marvelous and soaring song of praise attributed to St. Ambrose, which gathers biblical history and our own world in one grand hymn, nimbly leaping across the centuries to assert, "This is the night" of Passover, original and renewed. The deacon does not sing, "This is the anniversary of that night long ago" or "This celebration here and now reminds us of the event there and then," but simply, powerfully, even disconcertingly "This is the night." This is the night in which the Passover and the Exodus and the death and resurrection of Christ and the Holy Communion through the centuries are all joined in one simultaneous event as all time is made contemporary and as Egypt and Sinai and Jerusalem and Rome and New York and Bangalore and each parish coalesce and become one.

4. Finally, song can teach us something about the nature of liturgical language, for it is a language that is not natural to us; it is a language that we must learn. What Victor Zuckerkandl says of music may also be said of the liturgy:

To him who opens himself without reservation to symbols, their meaning will gradually become clear of itself. The Chinese who hears mere noise in our music has not yet given the symbols sufficient opportunity to impart to him the significance they contain.[45]

(And, we might add, still more tellingly, Westerners who give Asian symbols a similar opportunity can find in them equal riches.) Music can teach us patience in learning a new and unfamiliar language that is not immediately apprehended by everyone.

We can begin learning this new language by attending to the relationship between a voice and a hearer. Mark Booth describes it:

> The voice of another person who is not, like an actor in a play would be, addressing his voice overtly to some other specific person, a voice without dramatic context, presents itself as a medium of communication from someone else to me. As the flat eyes in a painting or the finger of Uncle Sam point at the observer, undirected spoken words direct themselves straight toward any listener. One may read with equanimity a sign saying "Exit" or even "Abandon hope, all ye who enter here." But when the stooge on television delivers a commercial message, I surrender an involuntary smile of social agreeableness; when the recording at the Los Angeles airport admonishes against parking, it is very difficult to proceed to park. Words from a voice are privileged in their power to arrest attention. We appoint ourselves the addressees.
>
> We have the same impulse with sung words, attending to them as if they were spoken, and spoken to us in particular.[46]

The separation between performer and audience dissolves. The singer sings for the audience both in the sense of being in front of the listeners as well as singing on their behalf. The experience of song makes the audience more than listeners.

> Because song comes to us in a voice, without dramatic context, to pass through the consciousness of the listener, it fosters some degree of identification between singer and audience.... When this ideal is achieved, when this fusion is entered into by listeners, the performance is *for* the audience in the second sense: the singer's words are sung for us in that he says something that is also said

somehow in extension *by* us, and we are drawn into the state, the pose, the attitude, the self offered by the song.[47]

This, as Booth notes, is also a description of what happens in ritual. The individual enters into a common pattern of thought, attitude, emotion, and achieves it by concert with society. "When we hear the song, we are the concert."[48] Moreover, a song is heard as if said by us. In a song in which the singer addresses a second person, the audience identifies with the speaking voice. The effect is in fact so compelling as to overcome the difference of gender: a man who hears a woman singing a declaration of love generally identifies himself with the declarer rather than the beloved. So it is with the language of the liturgy. The words are there to speak for us, for us to accommodate ourselves to, to appropriate as our own. We attend to the liturgy not to hear ourselves but to hear the voices of others in whom we can come to know our own humanity. We attend to the liturgy most of all to listen to the voice of Another, who leads us out of ourselves and into a profound communion with him and with one another.

In Elie Wiesel's novel *The Gates of the Forest*, Gregor, a survivor of the Holocaust, now in New York years later, goes to Brooklyn to a Hassidic celebration and there meets a wise old rabbi. The spiritless survivor asks the teacher, "Make me able to cry." The Rebbe shook his head. "That's not enough. I shall teach you to sing." After midnight the Rebbe suddenly demands a Hungarian song. The only song he can elicit is a "barracks-room drinking song, vulgar, obscene, and blasphemous," but with the encouragement of the Rebbe the song, tentatively begun, grows firmer until "at the end all the multitude took up the song." The song transported Gregor to a place far away "where he, who had been killed by the god of war, was awaiting him."[49] The Rebbe had accomplished a miracle, and he had accomplished it through song.

Words can be elevated into poetry, and poetry can be elevated into song, and song can be elevated into wordless music. As poetry may be understood to be perfected speech, so music can be understood to be perfected utterance, and, as is true of speech, "the perfection of music is silence."[50]

In James Joyce's short story *The Dead*, Gabriel Conroy strains his ear to listen to the stillness after a song sung by the tenor Bartell D'Arcy. "*Distant Music* he would call the picture if he were a painter."[51] The stillness after a song speaks of completion, indeed of the poignancy of perfection and repose. But there is also in music something that is beyond the hearing of the ear, that for which one does not have to wait until the song is finished, the fugue completed. John Keats in his "Ode on a Grecian Urn" wrote,

> Heard melodies are sweet, but those unheard
> Are sweeter; therefore, ye soft pipes, play on;
> Not to the sensual ear, but, more endear'd,
> Pipe to the spirit dittites of no tone. . . .

If Keats had in mind only the beauty of imagined music he would have told the pipes to be quiet, to cease their interference with the sweeter melodies he hears in his mind and imagination. But instead he asks the soft pipes to "play on" to the spirit "ditties" without tones. Keats may have reference to the music of the spheres, the inaudible harmony of surpassing beauty. Moreover, as the music plays, the mind attends to an unheard melody of the moving patterns that reveal the buried insides of things, that make sense of the surface, sights, sounds of the world. One hears sounds, but one cannot be said accurately to hear patterns or attitudes. These must be thought or heard with the mind and so may be described as "unheard melodies."

Every serious work of art presents not a copy of reality but a thoughtful reflection that composes the familiar surface into something more deeply meaningful.[52] Music is composed of sounds and sound shapes, but there is only noise if we do not hear the forms within the sounds, as we sometimes do not when listening to music from an alien culture.[53] Meaning is never identical with what the work of art says or depicts or sings. Even when it utters truths, the enacted meaning, the unseen picture, the unheard melody is never the same as the statement of its meaning.[54] The meaning of a poem can be described in words, but it can never be reduced to words; and so it is with all forms of art, including the liturgy.

> In resisting the chaos of enslaved echoes into which our lives are forever falling, art transmits to us the shaping power of the unseen, the unheard, and the unspoken that enables expression to take place.[55]

In a word, art, and most of all music, brings us into the presence of God, the most ancient of all mysteries out of whose primal silence the Word was spoken and whose unheard melody underlies, orders, and preserves in life all the universe.

Chapter Five

THE NECESSITY OF CONTINUITY

~ ✠ ~

I N THE FINE ARTS the word "conservation" is used to refer to the preservation of a work of art from harm or decay. The preservation often involves restoration, the removal of damaging accretions, sometimes added by those who, despite their good intentions, did not understand the effect of what they were doing: for example, applying to a painting a protective varnish that in time darkened and cracked and damaged the underlying paint. The liturgy requires similar conservation, the removal of accretions that obscure, distort, or falsify the basic intention, thereby allowing the work to shine forth in its intended beauty and to speak with greater clarity and power. Such conservation makes possible responsible criticism, evaluation, and reflection. The liturgy, like all works of art, requires conservation. This is primarily the work and concern of specialists in the field. It also needs to be observed, however, that the liturgy itself is conservative, and this aspect is the concern of all who use it. Like an antique cabinet the liturgy has a patina that softens and enhances its beauty, adding a depth of character and preserving a long and diverse record of its use. The liturgy thus functions as a conservator for humanity, preserving from loss or distortion those perspectives, experiences, and discoveries that have been formative of the faith and thereby preserving us from the forces of decay and ruin.

In his study of the Gospel according to St. Mark, *The Genesis of Secrecy*, Frank Kermode takes the puzzling passages in the Gospel, rather than its clearer sections, as central to an understanding of its author's purpose. He uses as an example the incident of the young man who flees naked leaving his cloak in the astonished soldiers' hands (Mark 14:51–52). This curious detail is not integrated into the narrative. We are not told who the "young man" is or why his departure is significant. Kermode's point is that such a break in the coherence of the narrative does not imperil the meaning of the story but rather adds to it. The event has special meaning precisely because it is puzzling. An anomalous incident cannot be explained satisfactorily as a reference to a historical happening, as an example of the rough and disordered nature of life itself, as part of the sources with which the evangelist is working. Narratives are integrated wholes, and allowing such an unintegrated detail to stand is contrary to narrative interest. Kermode argues that the author's intention is therefore to create in the narrative a sense of greater meaning than that which is immediately available. It is so too with perplexing aspects of the liturgy, those elements seemingly no longer relevant to modern life and experience. For example, relics of Roman papal practice such as the elaborate entrance rite common to the Roman, Lutheran, and Anglican rites, consisting of entrance hymn or psalm, Kyrie, Gloria in Excelsis, and collect, may yet retain value in that they suggest the antiquity of the rite and its long history. Only those items that are clearly contrary to a modern understanding of the central purpose and teaching of the Gospel are to be discarded, for such are indeed harmful and their actual mischief far outweighs any potential historical memory. One example is the ancient practice of baptizing first men, then children, and then women. Such denigration of women to third class is plainly intolerable in the celebration of the sacrament of initiation into the body of Christ in whom there is neither male nor female, slave nor free, but in whom all are one.

Liturgy, holding within itself the record of its long heritage, is a conservative discipline. Its conservatism must, however, be carefully understood. It is not just negative activity, defending the status quo and rejecting any movement, change, or alteration of what has become familiar and comfortable. For that is the road to death. The liturgy is conservative in the best sense of the term: preserving the fullness of the past experience in order to keep its discoveries available for the present and the future. It presents ways of being open to the present and to the future and responding to their challenges while keeping faith with the past. It opposes the secular, that is, an attitude that embraces uncritically the interest of the present age (*saeculum*), and it is persistently religious (*re-ligare/re-legere*), by tying humanity back to its origins, making connections, preserving a clear sense of roots and a heritage of growth and discovery.

The Long Perspective

Bishop Eivind Berggrav observed in connection with his "homecoming to the woods,"

> I was elated over the reforestation plan for North-Norway.... That it has national economic importance goes without saying; but I have faith that it will be a balancing factor culturally and spiritually.... The forest grows slowly. Life at short sight is exciting — I don't complain of that — but the human and the cultural must take a long view — enduring — and become reconciled to the fact that we do not immediately gather the profit. The woods cultivate men's minds. It gives the long, but sure, perspective of growth.[1]

The liturgy, like Berggrav's woods, confronts us with the longer perspective against which we measure ourselves. It is not the first task of liturgy to speak what is immediately applicable to individual lives and present concerns. This may surely come, but the starting point is less greedy and self-centered. Worship, we learn, is a gift that is grandly and gladly given by creatures to their Creator without thought of its benefit to the worshippers who render it. Liturgy and liturgical change is like reforestation: we do not immediately gather the profit. Indeed, the present generation may not gather the profit. A study of liturgy teaches the long view.

The relevance of Berggrav's forest for the understanding of the liturgy is not only the required long perspective. There is also the "mysterious likeness between word and seed"[2] that recalls biblical metaphors and the parables of the sower[3] and the mustard tree[4] and the Johannine likening of Christ himself to a seed ("Unless a grain of wheat falls into the earth and dies, it remains just a single grain; but if it dies, it bears much fruit," John 12:24) and the appreciation at the beginning of Genesis and in Isaiah 55 of the latent energy inherent in a word that, when released, gives life and growth. Seeds are tiny centers of potential life that under favorable conditions swell and sprout and grow. Words also seem small, even insignificant, but contain the vigor and promise of vitality and stimulation and development.[5]

In part because of our youth America is impatient with history, tradition, the long view. Henry Ford's celebrated remark that "history is bunk" may be a useful correction when past ways of doing things and

traditional ways of thinking shrink our minds and shrivel our imagina-
tions like the Neanderthal neighbor in Robert Frost's "Mending Wall"
who will not go behind his father's saying and likes it so well that he
says it again, "Good fences make good neighbors." He repeats unthink-
ingly and uncritically what he heard from his father even though, as
Frost's speaker knows, the old saying that made sense when both farms
raised livestock no longer has meaning now that "He is all pine and I
am apple orchard." The neighbor will not consider the insistent question of the speaker, "Why?" Misused and misunderstood, the past can
paralyze. But used with imagination and insight history can liberate and
enlarge our view and encourage responsible growth and development.
Tradition, T. S. Eliot observed, is "the means by which the vitality of the
past enriches the life of the present." Tradition cannot mean standing
still.[6]

Put simply, without liturgical tradition Christians are deprived of the
necessary language by which faith is formed and motivated. A sense
of continuity is necessary to help guard against an irresponsible and
directionless flight into chance and momentary sensation or wandering
in the aimless byways of immediate relevance.

The Moon and the Mystery

The varying date of Easter is a mystery that encourages worshippers
to take the long view. The yearly variation in the date seems at first
glance to be an unnecessary inconvenience. Easter can come as early
as March 22 and as late as April 25. The festival falls on its extremes
only rarely. It last fell on March 22 in 1818 and will not do so again
until 2285; it last happened on April 25 in 1943 and will not do so
again until 2038. Not uncommonly Easter comes toward the end of
March, and this seems an inconvenience to merchants. The problem
could be eliminated if Christianity would adopt the proposal advanced
by a committee of the League of Nations in 1926 that each year Easter
be celebrated on the Sunday following the second Saturday in April.
(Why, in the interest of simplicity, a straightforward "first Sunday in
April" or "second Sunday in April" wasn't selected was not explained.)
For those who care deeply about the continuity that Judaism and Christianity represent, however, the proposal for a fixed date for Easter is a
bad idea.

The date of Easter has been a problem to Christianity from the start. At the beginning of the Christian movement in the Roman province of Asia the Christians in their own way continued the traditional cele‐ bration of the Passover. Easter was celebrated on the fourteenth of the lunar month Nisan, the beginning of Passover, the date of the killing of the Passover lamb. In the Gospel of St. John, Jesus, whom John the Baptist called "the lamb of God," is understood to have been crucified at the same time as the Passover lamb was being killed, Nisan 14 (John 19:31, 36). As John the Evangelist understands it, the crucifixion was not a tragedy but was in fact "the hour" of Jesus' glorification (John 12:23–33). Crucifixion and resurrection were originally joined as one event (which for John included also the ascension and the sending of the Spirit.) The one great central festival was the celebration of the redemptive death of Christ.

Polycarp of Smyrna (died ca. 156) followed this tradition. Polycrates of Ephesus (died ca. 200), corroborated by Irenaeus (as reported by Eu‐ sebius in his *History of the Church*[7] of about 325) traces this tradition of celebrating Easter on Nisan 14 back to Philip the Apostle and to the apostle and evangelist John, who reclined on the Lord's breast at the Last Supper. The Asian Christians who followed John's tradition were called Quartodecimians (fourteenthers), observers of the fourteenth of Nisan. Their divergence from the practice of the rest of Christianity was already noted by Pope Xystus I (ca. 115).

The larger part of Christianity, for which Xystus spoke, placed em‐ phasis on the Synoptic chronology, which understood the Last Supper, rather than the crucifixion, to have occurred on the day of the killing of the Passover lamb. Death and resurrection were separated, and Easter was celebrated on Sunday, "the first day of the week" (Matt. 28:1; Mark 16:2; Luke 24:1; John 20:1) following Passover, whatever the date of that Sunday. (Already the movement away from Judaism had begun; the thin end of the wedge had been inserted between Passover and Easter.)

The Council of Nicaea in 325 settled the Easter question against the Quartodecimians and in favor of the Roman practice. But the calcula‐ tion of what Sunday was to be regarded as Easter continued to vary. At first Christianity simply followed the Jewish calculation of Passover, but growing hostility between the two communities led Christians to make their own calculations independently. Easter Day therefore is al‐ ways the Sunday after the full moon that occurs on or after the spring equinox on March 21 "according to ecclesiastical computation." This full moon may happen on any date between March 21 and April 18 inclusive. If the full moon occurs on a Sunday, Easter Day is the Sunday following. Thus Easter Day cannot be earlier than March 22 or later than April 25. It is to be noted that this full moon is not the astronomical full moon but a liturgical construct and approximation, an "ecclesiastical full moon."

The *computus*, as the calculation of the date of Easter is called, for most of Christian history was part of the training of the priest, and directions regarding the computation were included in the missal. The *Book of Common Prayer* retains the section (pp. 880–83), but the *Lutheran Book of Worship*, unlike its predecessor books, has omitted even the Easter table.

The earliest known Easter table is by Hippolytus, made in 222 and based on a sixteen-year lunar cycle; it is inscribed on the throne on which his statue sits in the Lateran museum. The next Easter table is *De pascha computus* of 243, formulated by an African scholar to correct a three-day error in Hippolytus's table. Anatolius, bishop of Laodicaea, in about 258 introduced a nineteen-year cycle, which was adopted in Alexandria by Cyril in about 450 and through the translation of Dionysus "the little" (*Exiguus*), ca. 525, became the standard. Nevertheless, there were other tables devised by such people as the Venerable Bede in 731 dating from the Incarnation, Helperic of Auxerre in the ninth century, John of Sacrobosco, Robert Groseteste, and Roger Bacon. There was also the Celtic calculation based on an eighty-four-year cycle.

Christianity was going its own way, independent of Judaism, but certain ties remained. In the Eastern churches, which in many ways still retain a strikingly Jewish character, Easter must follow Passover. Maintaining the connection between Passover, the central festival of Judaism, and Easter, the central festival of Christianity, is one reason why a fixed date is a bad idea. It would sever that faint but still surviving relationship.

There is a second reason why a fixed date for Easter is undesirable. Passover and therefore Easter are related to the moon. It is in this relationship of both Passover and Easter to the moon that their earliest origins lie. The roots of the common celebration disappear into the clouds of the very distant past. The roots reach back to Neolithic times and indeed come near the beginning of the human race. The moon, the first of the creatures to die but also the first to live again, is close to the source of human religious impulse and thought, and for millennia what Eliade calls "the lunar perspective" shaped human response and existence.[8] The cycle of the moon approximates the menstrual cycle. The phases of the moon — appearance, increase, wane, disappearance, and reappearance after three nights of darkness — give a rhythm that governs short intervals of the week and the month (Swinburne called the moon "the mother of months"[9]) and also more extended durations, for the moon tells of what Eliade calls a "universal becoming,"[10] which gives optimism and hope, for the disappearance of the moon is never final. The light of the moon partakes of darkness and thus is at once mortal and immortal.[11] One sees in individuals, as in the moon, birth, growth, aging, and disappearance. One sees in humanity itself, as in the moon, according to many and widespread ancient myths, appearance, growth, decay, and disappearance in a deluge or cataclysm. But the message of the moon is that the disappearance is never permanent. In fact, a periodic death seems necessary for the regeneration of the moon, the individual, the race, the cosmos. The moon is the celestial sign of the mystery of rebirth,[12] self-consuming and self-renewing, "reborn of its own substance."[13] So the universe has a cyclical structure of "eternal return,"[14] but it is no mere repetition, for the cycles and interlocking structures proclaim an unfinished task, a universal becoming, always drawing us on beyond the horizon to something more. Philip Wheelwright has observed that humanity

> lives always on the verge, always on the borderland of a something more.... Even when — perhaps especially when — we succeed in allaying the grosser forms of uneasiness, the sense of a beyond and the urge to wonder about it remain.
>
> Indeed, the intimation of a something more, a beyond the horizon, belongs to the very nature of consciousness.... To be conscious is not just to be; it is to mean, to intend, to point beyond oneself, to testify that some kind of beyond exists and to be ever on the verge of entering into it.[15]

Symbol, myth, ritual, liturgy encourage and enable us to find suggestive patterns in the world in which and by which we live and also to see through the cracks of the visible universe[16] to find a deeper harmony.

Time governed and measured by the phases of the moon is bound up with the reality of life and nature, rain and the tides, the time of sowing, the menstrual cycle, in such an intimate way that it is what Eliade calls "living time."[17] A whole series of phenomena belonging to totally different "cosmic levels" is ordered according to the rhythms of the moon or is under their influence. Since the Neolithic age at least, with the discovery of agriculture, the same symbolism has linked together the moon, the sea and the waters, rain and dew, the fertility of women and animals, plant life, human destiny after death, and the rituals of initiation. The moon measures, and it also unifies.

It is important to notice in this context that a sacred object, whether for Stone Age people or for modern Christians, is not honored or adored in itself but rather for what it reveals of the sacred, because it reveals and participates in ultimate reality.[18] Think of the crucifix, think of the bread and wine in the Holy Communion, and think also of the moon.

Eliade, following many other students of the history of religion, identifies several areas connected with, indeed governed, by the moon. (Keep Passover and Easter in mind.)

1. The moon governs the waters because rain and dew and tides are subject to its rhythms. Floods may be understood to correspond to the three days of darkness or "death" of the moon, but, like the moon, their destruction is never final, for it takes place "under the seal of the moon and the waters,"[19] which are preeminently the sign of growth and regeneration. A flood destroys old and worn-out forms and clears them away, making room for a new humanity and a new history. There is pain and there is loss, but there is hope and renewal too.

2. The moon is connected with vegetation. It is the dispenser of the night dews by which the world of vegetation is refreshed.[20] Vegetation is subject to the same recurring cycles governed by the moon's movements. Both moon and plants undergo death, but they do so as rest and regeneration, never as a conclusion.[21] French peasants, even today, sow at the time of the new moon, but they prune their trees and pick their vegetables when the moon is on the wane, presumably in order not to go against the rhythms of nature by damaging a living organism when nature's forces are on the upward swing.[22] Several farmers' calendars in the United States give similar advice.

3. The moon governs fertility in animals as well as in plants. The unalterable character of the moon is "the prerogative of fertility, of recurring creation, of inexhaustible life."[23] Wherever the horns of the

oxen are found in Neolithic cultures, they denote the presence of the Great Goddess of fertility. The horn is the image of the new moon: it brings to mind a crescent, and both horns together (moon and ox) represent two crescents or the complete career of the moon.[24] Certain animals become symbols or even "presences" of the moon because their shape or their behavior is reminiscent of that of the moon. Among them is the snake, because according to Aristotle and Pliny the snake has as many coils as the moon has days, and because it sloughs off its skin and is reborn.[25] There are, Fraser and Eliade tell us, innumerable myths telling the disastrous story of how the serpent stole the immortality given by a god to humans.[26]

Because the moon is the source of fertility and also governs the menstrual cycle, it has been personified as the "master of women." The snake as a lunar animal and as an epiphany of the moon shares this character with the moon and is called "the husband of all women." So a great many peoples have thought that the moon in the form of a man or a serpent copulates with their women. In a great number of traditions the moon, women, and snakes are joined in the large pattern of moon-rain-fertility-woman-serpent-death-periodic regeneration.[27]

4. The moon is the first of the dead, dark for three nights; its death, however, is not an extinction but a change to a new level of existence.[28] What happens to the moon and to the earth, as agricultural peoples came to know it, must happen to individuals as well, for there is life in death. Widespread traditional ideas see the moon as the land of the dead and the receiver and regenerator of souls.[29]

5. So the moon is prominent in initiation rituals, for they consist of a ritual death followed by a rebirth of a new person. Moreover, if initiation can be looked upon as a death, death can be looked upon as an initiation. This "becoming" is the lunar order of things, and the moon, a living creature, is not just the measure but the measurer who feeds, blesses, and makes fruitful, who receives the dead, initiates and purifies — itself, like all life, in a perpetual state of rhythmic becoming.[30] The moon weaves all life[31] into a wonderful web of intimacy and joined meanings[32] in which every piece fits and nothing is isolated from the others. Everything hangs together, everything is connected and makes up a cosmic whole.[33]

The sun in the early mythologies of the moon-bull was conceived of as a blazing, destructive deity, a terrible force, as indeed it is in the tropics.[34] The moon, on the other hand, represents the principle of life in the broadest and most inclusive sense. It is the governor and measure of the life-creating rhythm of the womb and thereby of time through which beings come and go.[35] It is the ruler of the mystery of birth and death, for both are aspects of one state of being. It is the controller of the tides and of the dew that falls at night to refresh the grass on which the cattle graze, the source of the waters of life, the ruler of the oceans that surround this island earth.[36]

Now, with these lunar images in mind, one may profitably turn to the images of Easter (and Passover, for Christians should not think about their Passover without recalling the original festival). Eliade calls the time governed by the moon "living time." Easter also marks living time, for it is that festival that is at the center of the Christian year and that gives Paschal character to days and observances and times throughout the year.

1. The moon governs the waters. The principal image of Passover-Easter is the passage of the Red Sea, which the church understands to be a type of baptism. The water of the sea, like the water of baptism, destroys the old and opens the way to a new people with a new history before them. At creation, at the flood, at the exodus, and at baptism life comes from the water. A new people is born.

2. The moon is connected with vegetation. An image of Israel — old and new — is the vineyard described in Isaiah 5, the canticle following the eighth lesson (Isa. 5:1–2b, 7a) in the Lutheran form of the Easter Vigil. Moreover, Jesus refers to himself as the vine and his followers as the branches (John 15:1–8, the Gospel for the Fifth Sunday of Easter in Year B.) Passover and Easter both have their focus in a meal as the celebrants feast on the fruits of the earth, grain and grapes.

3. The moon governs fertility. A central image of Christian baptism describes the font as a womb, fruitful and bearing a great number of new Christians. Moreover, the association of moon and woman and serpent and death surely reminds Christians of the story of creation in the first three chapters of Genesis, which in the Lutheran rite is the first reading at the Easter Vigil, setting the celebration of Easter in the context of the history of the world.

4. The moon dies, is dark for three nights, and is reborn. It anticipates and shares in the message of Passover-Easter of death and life, the dearly bought victory of resurrection and life.

5. The moon is prominent in initiation rituals, and Easter, the festival of deliverance and life, is the premier occasion for baptism in the

Christian church as individuals pass through the waters, drowning the old nature, and emerge as newborn Christians.

The moon, Eliade says, shows us our true human condition, for in its rhythmic pattern is both *pathos* and consolation.[37] The pattern is one of change and is at the same time disturbing and consoling. Individual manifestations of life are so frail that they can disappear altogether (the Ash Wednesday theme); they can nonetheless be restored. The message is "harsh and merciful,"[38] that is, in Lutheran terminology, it is composed of Law and Gospel.

The point of all this accumulated association is that the suggestion that we fix a date for Easter, such as the second Sunday in April, is too facile. In view of the enormous symbolic tradition that is joined under the figure of the moon, such an invariable celebration is not only unwise, it is indeed unwelcome to those who cherish the long memory of the human race.

The ancient association of moon and Passover and Easter, apparently obsolete and expendable, yields a wealth of rich and suggestive insight, joining what Christians know to what humankind has recognized for much of the millennia of its history. Maintaining the association of Easter and the moon is healthful, deeply answering primordial impulses and giving a satisfaction even more profound than the intellect can provide.

There is an approach to experience that divides the world neatly into pairs of opposites: male-female, life-death, true-false, good-evil. Mythologically this view has been expressed by the solar image. The sun is dependable, rising every morning without fail and setting every evening without interruption. It is bright, clear, always the same, dividing day from night, light from dark, truth from error, sight from blindness. Such an approach has a seductive, clear, and no-nonsense character to it. In contrast to this solar view, however, mythology has usually cherished a lunar view in which dark and light interact in one sphere, as in the moon, and pairs of opposites are not separated but joined together. So truth and fiction can be joined as in Jesus' parables. Life and death are seen as parts of one whole picture, as in the Passion of Christ, his life-giving death being the death of death. Good and evil are unknowable apart from each other, and in the striking phrase from the Exsultet the fall of Adam was a "happy sin" (*felix culpa*) because it made necessary the full revelation of the boundlessness of the redeeming love of God who entered into the world to live and die as one of us.

The Conservation of Tradition

There may be value in what we do not understand. The story is told that Reinhold Niebuhr once asked his close friend Abraham Heschel, "Why do you observe the dietary laws?" The wise rabbi replied, "My friend, I will give you a strange answer. I observe the dietary laws because I do not understand them."[39] Long before, in the eleventh century, Anselm, archbishop of Canterbury, spoke of "faith seeking understanding:" "I do not seek to understand so that I may believe; but I believe so that I may understand."[40] In the twentieth century Paul Ricoeur has taken that ancient phrase and has given it a double force: "We must understand in order to believe, but we must believe in order to understand."[41] He speaks to the modern mind. We assume that understanding has priority and that we must understand in order to believe, that we must clear away obscurity and clutter and magic and myth so that modern people can come without hindrance to faith, moving by a direct and unobstructed path. To a certain degree that is so. (Ricoeur allows that "we must understand in order to believe.") Unnecessary obscurity, that which is clearly obsolete (the Tudor language of "thou" and "thy" and "thee" for example) may well be expendable. But we go further and seek to make our worship say what we think it ought to say so that it will speak to modern people in a language that we think they will understand. And that is a dangerous thing to do, for in so doing we often lose the voice of the Gospel that is over against us, confronting us from another place, speaking from an unsuspected perspective, calling into question our easy assumptions and favorite ideas. The point is not to have a Bible and a liturgy that say what we mean but to have a Bible and a liturgy that require us to mean what they say. So Ricoeur with Anselm insists that "we must believe in order to understand."

In the eighty-fifth tract of the *Tracts for the Times* John Henry Newman wrote, "Let us maintain, before we have proved. This seeming paradox is the secret of happiness." Thomas Henry Huxley dismissed Newman's insight as "ecclesiasticism, the championship of a foregone conclusion."[42] But Huxley does not understand the important point that Newman was getting at. For Newman, who was not talking about science, we first of all maintain, that is, preserve, tend the tradition. Newman does not say that the matter is therefore settled, as if there was nothing more to be said. He does not say that we should not or need not prove. (He apparently means "prove" in the sense of probe, test, examine critically.) Newman says that we ought to begin by maintaining, keeping the tradition that we have received, and then probe, test, prove. It is not unlike a marriage. We make the marriage vow first, and then we grow into an ever-deeper understanding of what that solemn promise means. Thus in marriage and in religion happiness, blessedness, contentment is achieved. "This seeming paradox is the secret of happiness."

The liturgy of the church, attentively heard, enlarges our perception and understanding. As a work of human imagination it accomplishes what Shelley ascribed to poetry:

Poetry enlarges the circumference of the imagination by replenishing it with thoughts of ever-new delight.[43]

Liturgy too "enlarges the circumference of the imagination," filling the new space thus created with challenging and disturbing ideas, insights, and images, such as the full moon at Easter.

The American Roman Catholic theologian John S. Dunne speaks of the Christian religion as a mystery, not because it is bewildering and incomprehensible but because it is an inexhaustible source of answerable questions, a mine of discovery. Mystery for him means not unintelligibility "but inexhaustible intelligibility."[44] Early in the twentieth century G. K. Chesterton declared his delight in the Creed for, despite its (to some) forbidding complexity and theological precision, it showed that the Christian faith was "rich in discoveries":

When once one believes in a creed, one is proud of its complexity, as scientists are proud of the complexity of science. It shows how rich it is in discoveries. If it is right at all, it is a compliment to say that it's elaborately right.[45]

There is in Christianity, as in all religions worthy of attention, a willing acceptance of that which lies beyond rational understanding.

At the beginning of the sixth chapter of Genesis there is preserved a most peculiar story. It has to do with "the sons of the gods" (who cannot here be angels as they can be understood elsewhere in the Hebrew Bible because angels are sexless beings); they have children by certain human women who took their fancy, thereby producing a race of giants. The Jewish scholar E. A. Speiser comments,

The undisguised mythology of this isolated fragment makes it
not only atypical of the Bible as a whole but also puzzling and
controversial in the extreme.[46]

The peculiar passage is unlike anything else in the entire Bible, and
from the biblical perspective it makes no sense at all. It seems to have
floated in from some place like ancient Greece where such stories were
common. And yet somehow it was preserved in the Hebrew Bible.
Those nameless (although not letterless — the passage is by J) editors
of Genesis did not discard from their treasure of stories this one even
though it did not fit with the rest. Such was their respect for the traditions they were dealing with that they retained even something that
they perhaps could not understand. Because of their reverence for the
tradition this bit of undisguised mythology was saved despite its anomalous character, and we can appreciate its function in the Genesis story
even if its original meaning is lost to us.

So Speiser can make convincing sense out of the inclusion of this odd
passage. It seems to have been included here just before the account of
the flood as an example of the human morbid imagination. The editor
and presumably the readers would be filled with horror at the depravity
of such a story. It is a "moral indictment" and "a compelling motive for
the forthcoming disaster." "A world that could entertain such notions
deserved to be wiped out."[47] Thus some aspects of this puzzling story
can be understood and its position as a prelude to the deluge seems
clear. Had the ancient biblical editors discarded what they might have
considered obsolete, outmoded, or even false, we would be the poorer
and so would their story.

So too with the ancient association of Passover, Easter, and the
moon. There are riches here to be pondered with profit. The long
view challenges our addiction to the immediately relevant and con-
soles us with a confidence in that which is enduringly dependable. The
Grande Chartreuse, a monastery high in the French Alps, was established in 1084 by St. Bruno, the founder of the stringently ascetic order,
the Carthusians. The monastery fascinated English Protestant poets of
the nineteenth century, who found its stability enviable in a time of
eroded certainties. William Wordsworth, who had visited the monastery in 1790, wrote of it in *The Prelude* (1800). In response to the zeal
of the French Revolution Nature says,

> Your impious work forbear, perish what may,
> Let this one temple last, be this one spot
> Of earth devoted to eternity! (6.433–35)

Matthew Arnold, who like many Victorians was distressed by the "melancholy, long, withdrawing roar" of the Sea of Faith that he mourned in *Dover Beach,* visited the monastery in 1851 and wrote,

> Wandering between two worlds, one dead,
> The other powerless to be born,
> With nowhere yet to rest my head,
> Like these, on earth I wait forlorn.
> Their faith, my tears, the world deride —
> I come to shed them at their side (85–90)
>
> ... these
> Last of the people who believe! (111–12)

At the end of the century, the dissolute Ernest Dowson was more confident of their timeless witness. In *Carthusians* (1891) he wrote,

> Ye shall prevail at last! Surely ye shall prevail!
>   Your silence and austerity shall win at last;
> Desire and mirth, the world's ephemeral lights shall fail,
>   The sweet star of your queen is never overcast. (25–28)
>
> Pray for our heedlessness, O dwellers with the Christ!
>   Though the world fall apart, surely ye shall prevail. (35–36)

(The envied stability lay in the faith and practice of the monks, not their monastery. The present building dates only from 1678, and the monks were compelled to leave France in 1903.)

The value of what we do not understand can speak still to a time yearning for mystery and wonder, an age that swallows stories of ancient astronauts building the pyramids, that clutches astrology to its heart, that listens to what claim to be ancient voices speaking through a modern Californian. We laugh at these examples, as well we should, for they are of no social or religious use. Listen to Chesterton again:

> The real trouble with this world of ours is not that it is an
> unreasonable world, not even that it is a reasonable one. The
> commonest kind of trouble is that it is nearly reasonable, but not
> quite. Life is not an illogicality; yet it is a trap for the logicians. It

looks just a little more mathematical and regular than it really is; its exactitude is obvious, but its inexactitude is hidden; its wildness lies in wait. It is this silent swerving from accuracy by an inch that is the uncanny element in everything. It seems a sort of secret treason in the universe. An apple or an orange is round enough to get itself called round, and yet is not round after all. The earth itself is shaped like an orange to lure some simple astronomer into calling it a globe. A blade of grass is called after the blade of a sword, because it comes to a point; but it doesn't. Everywhere in things there is this element of the quiet and incalculable. It escapes the rationalists, but it never escapes until the last moment.

... Whenever we find that there is something odd in Christian theology, we shall generally find that there is something odd in the truth.[48]

If then one listens attentively to the liturgy with ears and heart and mind and indeed even with the eyes, one can learn new and exciting things. Doors open on new questions, new ideas, new insights. What seemed hopelessly obsolete becomes suddenly contemporary. What was familiar and dull may one day, as one goes through it yet again, even by rote, mechanically and unfeelingly, suddenly open before one's eyes to reveal an unsuspected layer of meaning for that person at that moment in that person's life. A word or phrase or image may suddenly attack, perhaps jumping us from behind, perhaps opening in the mind slowly and inexorably. One tangled in the web of an adulterous affair, another struggling against addiction to a drug hear, for example, the seemingly bland and expected words of a prayer,

> O God, you know that we cannot withstand the dangers which surround us. Strengthen us in body and spirit so that, with your help, we may be able to overcome the weakness that our sin has brought upon us.[49]

The old Leonine collect deriving from the precarious state of the church in the collapse of the Roman Empire and the barbarian destruction takes on new and personal meaning in the late twentieth century: an acknowledgement of our inability to manage on our own, a confession of our responsibility for the plight in which we find ourselves, and a prayer for God's strength for our body as well as our mind. A liturgy so charged with potential can open its riches for scholars and for others as well, intellectuals and ordinary people, the wise and the simple alike.

Indeed, there are explosives hidden in the liturgy as in the Bible, because the liturgy is so filled with the language and spirit and message of the Bible, and they may go off when we least expect. If we do not hold on to what we have inherited from the past we would deprive ourselves of the wisdom of those who have gone before us and who arrived at their knowledge and their formulations after great struggle and at great cost.

That may not boost the attendance in a struggling parish. It may not spread harmony in a divisive congregation or invigorate a moribund church. But it will make the Christian community more faithful to its past, more open to the promise of the future. The mark of an authentic church is that it is respectful of the accumulated treasure of the church's long experience, for in those images and symbols, many of which are older than we know, lie as yet undiscovered riches to be tended until we are ready to understand them. The preservation and employment of that life-giving treasure is what liturgy is all about.

Chapter Six

Worship and Christian Formation

~ ✠ ~

CHRISTIAN FORMATION begins in worship, for the liturgy is the church's school. Certain instructive features of the service that teach the peculiar language of the liturgy come to mind at once.

Liturgy as the Church's School

First, in the liturgy the church listens to the proclamation of Scripture. We hear the Bible read in substantial portions, usually three — Old Testament, Epistle, and Gospel, and often, especially with the three-year lectionary, these portions are read in continuous fashion. So week by week we learn and review the basic record of the faith. Moreover, we hear the Bible reflect and comment on itself as the responsorial psalm bridges the first and second lessons and as the Verse prepares for and welcomes the Gospel with an appropriate theme for the lection or the season. And, of course, we hear an application of some of what was read to present-day problems and concerns in the sermon, and, in the Lutheran rite, we hear a meditation on the themes of the lessons in the Hymn of the Day, which often makes further application of the readings to our lives. For all this to be effective, regular and attentive participation is required, especially in the light of the three-year lectionary. One must be in attendance every Sunday to get the full effect of this continuous instruction.

Second, in the seamless round of the church year we have our share in the life and work of Christ. We walk behind him in our pilgrim journey through this world toward the next. We are baptized with his baptism. We go with him into the desert for a time of testing and struggle to conform our lives to his. We walk with him along the *via dolorosa* and stand at the cross, shattered by the recognition that *we* crucified him. We look into his empty tomb and have there in its depths a glimpse of his future and ours. We rejoice in his new life, examining it from many perspectives throughout the Fifty Days and at their culmination receive his Spirit as our companion and guide. In the weeks and months that follow we learn of ways to manifest this new life that he shares with us, and we look toward "the end of all things and the day of his just judgment"[1] when he will "come again to judge the world in righteousness"[2] and reveal himself as the Lord of all nations, even as he once came in humility to share our life and lead us through the death and life of the water of baptism.

We hear the proclamation of Scripture. We make our yearly journey through the church year. Third, our instruction in the Christian faith is enriched each time we participate in the Great Thanksgiving that lifts our hearts and raises for our attention and praise the central assurances and promises of the faith, the heart of Christ's work: his saving death, triumphant resurrection, sending of the Spirit, and promise of his glorious Appearing. The great prayer of the Eucharist directs our hearts and minds and spirits in the attitudes proper to the Christian life: established in mutuality, unity, and peace —

> The Lord be with you
> *And also with you;*

lifted in exalted praise of God —

> Lift up your hearts
> *We lift them to the Lord;*

duty-bound to thanksgiving —

> Let us give thanks to the Lord our God
> *It is right to give him thanks and praise,*

always and everywhere, at all times and in all places — good and bad, joyful and sorrowful, exalting and depressing, in whatever state we find ourselves — by voice and by our lives giving thanks to the God of Israel who comes to save his people.

Thus week by week, in words and in actions, we have set before us again and again the essence of the Christian faith. We hear, we see, we do. We hear in word and song what God has done for us; we see in pictures and images and symbolic actions what God has done for us;

we by our actions share in what God has done for us and by our lives extend to others what God has done for us.

It happens over and over, week after week. Repetition is an important element of education. We learn by continual and constant review, wearing into our minds and into our very lives the memory and meaning of Christ's dying and rising.

In addition to the weekly commemoration there is something else, frequently overlooked. The central action of Holy Communion is supported and enriched with the regular round of Daily Prayer, the ancient regimen of prayer in the evening and in the morning, echoing the ordering of time in the creation account at the beginning of the Bible. The Holy Communion and its propers relate us to the cycle of the year; the Daily Prayer of the church binds us to another rhythm, the alternation of night and day, the basic measure of time. It reminds us children of a technological age, we who dwell in sealed, air-conditioned, brightly lit houses surrounded by the unsleeping world of television and newsgathering and traffic and entertainment that as little as we may be confronted by darkness and daylight we are in fact dependent on sunlight for our mental and physical health; that we with all the creatures share a rhythm of activity and rest, waking and sleeping. Daily Prayer reminds us in its quiet but insistent way that we are part of the natural world, inseparable from it, and that this environment requires our respect and care for our own good as well as the good of other creatures. For all of our sophistication, we are still children of the earth and share its rhythms.

Daily Prayer also enforces our connection with all humanity as we share in the nearly universal urge to pray at least in the evening as the sun sets, commending ourselves to God's care and protection, and in the morning as the sun rises, rejoicing in God's new mercies and the gift of life. Moreover, for those who have been captivated by the Christian story, evening and morning proclaim the death and resurrection of Christ and declare for all with ears to hear the paschal mystery of him who descended into the depths of darkness in order to bring life and immortality to light. St. Clement of Alexandria in his hymn for Holy Saturday, Easter Eve, binds the paschal passage and the diurnal rhythm together.

> Sunset to sunrise changes now,
> For God doth make his world anew:

> On the Redeemer's thorn-crowned brow
> The wonders of that dawn we view.[3]

Sunset and sunrise: these hours encourage and give shape to two complementary moods of worship — in the evening recollection and peace, and in the morning the joyful fulfillment of the night of waiting and preparation for the dawn of grace and opportunity.

Thus the liturgy provides the church with systematic and thorough instruction and review and in this way works the formation of Christians.

In all these ways the church acts as the keeper of memory, and by these repeated acts of remembering and thanksgiving the community tells the central story, preserving the remembrance of what has happened in those formative events that have created and given shape and content to what the church believes and teaches.

The liturgy rehearses and renews and deepens our understanding of the content of the faith, leading us ever more profoundly into the depths and heights and widest reaches of its mystery and power. In the regular repetition sometimes a new insight is given, old words are connected with new situations, familiar phrases touch our lives with a fresh hand. What has been made familiar by rote unexpectedly opens upon new and exciting meaning, and old words throb with new life and vigor.

The liturgy preserves the content of the faith. The liturgy also nourishes us in an appropriate response to that content, encouraging us by acts of praise and thanksgiving to make its words our words, its acts of praise our acts. When we are moved to praise, it provides us with appropriate words and songs and gestures to show forth our thanksgiving. That is to say, to its attentive participants, the liturgy in words and actions provides both motives for praise and a manner of praise.

Then the liturgy directs our attention beyond the assembly to the world of need lying at the church's doors and urges us to give convincing shape and expression to our thanksgiving "not only with our lips but in our lives,"[4] as St. Augustine said,[5] by living the new life that we have been given, no longer living for ourselves but for the one who has delivered us and given us life, and like him living for others.

In giving shape to the content and the response, to reveal the power and presence of the God who saves, the liturgy employs diverse images and metaphors and symbols. In so doing the liturgy broadens and deepens our understanding of language itself. Liturgy fosters an acquaintance with metaphor, the primal speech of religion. We are invited to reflect upon the marvel of language in all of its forms — spoken, written, sung, enacted — and to ponder the power of language to perform what it is spoken to accomplish. The language of the liturgy is in John Austin's phrase "performative language" and derives ultimately from the creative power of the language we hear at the opening of Genesis, "Let there be light, and there was light." The compression and multilayered richness of liturgical language reminds us that no human utterance is simple; the plainest remarks are freighted with nuance and suggestion and connotation. Moreover, the liturgy, like all of religion, deals with a particular application of metaphor in that compressed expression and concentrated language we call myth and its concomitant enactment in ritual.

Such symbolic depth, which encourages and enriches the imagination, requires the fullness of sensory perception to respond to it fully. Ear and eye and nose and hand and mouth all have their part to play in apprehending and responding to the richness of liturgical worship and that work of art which is the liturgy. In the words of Nelson Goodman,

> What we know through art is felt in our bones and nerves and muscles as well as grasped by our minds.... All the sensitivity and responsiveness of the organism participates in the invention and interpretation of symbols.[6]

Worship has traditionally with gladness embraced and reveled in seeing the light and color of the building and its furnishings and vestments, hearing the texts and the music of the liturgy, feeling the water of baptism, tasting the bread and wine of the Supper, smelling the aroma of wine and candles and incense; and worshippers have expressed their prayer and adoration by bowing the head, lifting or folding the hands, swaying or rocking their bodies, bending the knee, tracing the sign of the cross. All these are ways of recalling and preserving and proclaiming the central story, and this rich diversity and abundance encourage the fullness of our response in service to the world in which we live.

It is no simple task. We remember and give thanks for the primordial acts that give meaning to all subsequent activity, but we do so in the course of ongoing history, even in circumstances that call God's promises and even God's very existence into question. In a word, we live always in the shadow of the Holocaust. That and lesser experiences of loss, deprivation, and desolation make thanksgiving to God far from automatic or natural.

Because it has been remembered by people in diverse historical and cultural circumstances the manner of remembering has differed through the long history of Israel and Christianity, and all that has gone into the church's vast storehouses of treasured memory. Knowing that diversity, we are encouraged to engage the world in our time and keep the tradition a living tradition and with the story to touch the circumstances in which we live, to search for openings and to seek for places to build bridges and make connections.

Subjective-Objective Character

Such an understanding of liturgy runs head-on into certain pervasive modern attitudes. Robert Bellah and a team of social scientists have identified certain significant changes in modern culture;[7] at least two of them are most difficult for liturgists to deal with.

One is the privatization of reality. The individual has become the locus of meaning and value. In such a view, the individual has primary realty; society is second-order, a derived construct. The result is a loss of confidence in history, future vision, politics, social and cultural institutions. Most serious of all, religion becomes a radically private and individual matter. According to this view, one finds God first of all in the depths of one's soul and then, perhaps, becomes part of a congenial organization. Liturgy is useful only insofar as it facilitates one's personal encounter with the divine.

In addition to the privatization there is a second characteristic of modern society with which liturgists must contend, and that is a shift toward a kind of intimacy. Social complexity is being replaced by personal closeness and radical familiarity. So all sorts of strangers — bank tellers, telephone salespersons, clerks — presume to call us by our first names to make it seem that we are known and are their friend. A while ago I received a form letter from the company that owns my bank announcing a new line of credit. The letter began, "Dear Philip"; it was signed not with a corresponding first name but "James B. Durkin, Senior Vice President, Community Banking." I suppose that I am to be impressed that a senior vice president calls me by my first name. Most people apparently are pleased by this pseudo-personal touch. Formality to such people speaks of coldness, alienation, and so systems of etiquette, protocol, and manners are rejected. (Perhaps, one fears, nicknames are next if the computer can determine what they are: "Dear Bugsy." But that would not be done for that would border on real intimacy: nicknames are known only by those who really know you.) In a context like this the church becomes a friendly gathering place for individuals who have experienced the divine in their personal lives and who want warm personal congregations where they can feel the joy of belonging.

In such a system, the liturgy is no longer the public work that its etymology implies but a series of private, personal experiences of intimacy and relationship (I supplied once in a congregation where members after the service thanked me for "sharing" their service.) Liturgy is "worship experiences" in a place where the service begins not with the entrance hymn or "The grace of our Lord Jesus Christ" or "In the name of the Father, and of the Son, and of the Holy Spirit" but with a hearty "Good morning!" and its echo by the congregation, often repeated until its vigor and volume satisfy the presiding social director. Imagination and creativity seem, however, to be failing us; why is it that no one, as far as I know, has followed the benediction and dismissal with a hearty "Have a nice day!" (on feast days one may shout "Have a great day!")? The response would probably be "Take care."

The effect of the shift to the individual and to a kind of intimacy is heard in congregational complaints across the land[8] and is seen in those congregations whose leaders have surrendered to popular demand. Congregations are encouraged to replace traditional forms with their own "liturgies" using their everyday language.[9] A pastor observes, "The language needs to grow out of the weekday experience of the members of the congregation." (And, one is supposed to wonder, what would Justin Martyr, Hippolytus, or Gregory the Great know about that?) "It must be based on their own Christian faith, hope, and love...." Such virtues are apparently thought to spring full-blown in the hearts of each member without effort, instruction, or struggle. Young adults, we are told, sleep in on Sunday morning, explaining, "I'm just not motivated. There's nothing there for me." Luther, as so often, had the answer to that complaint. "Here stand the gracious and lovely words, 'This is my body, given *for you*,' 'This is my blood, poured out *for you* for the forgiveness of sins.' These words, I have said, are not preached to wood and stone but to you and me."[10] Speaking of those who receive the sacrament worthily Luther declared in the *Small Catechism*, that person "is truly worthy and well prepared who believes these words, 'for you' and 'for the forgiveness of sins.' "[11] The advice of the world is, build a liturgy on your own experience, for that is the measure of meaning. A layperson says of the language of worship, "Keep it easy to understand." Was it ever, can it ever be easy to understand the incarnation, the atonement, the paschal passage from death to life, the glorious appearing? The validity of liturgical language and any traditional forms are rejected, for

> unfortunately, the corporate recitation of words by a group does not provoke the memory, especially when the words are the same — or overly familiar — every week. Then the memory is not even needed; the mind is quite capable of focusing on other matters while the words emerge as if one is on automatic pilot.[12]

Here, then, is the crux of the issue. The culture tells us insistently that to be valid religious language and worship must be rooted in our experience and be straightforward, clear, simple, and fresh.

With the revision of the liturgy in the last third of the twentieth century has come a new emphasis on reducing not only the complexity but also the depth and subtlety of the liturgy and hymn texts so that, it was hoped, everyone in the congregation could readily understand what was being said and done and find immediate and clear relevance to individual situations. An overemphasis on the subjective and the relevant, however, renders the resulting text unchallenging and ultimately unsatisfying. Joseph Sittler, writing out of his long experience in the church and his profound understanding of the situation of humanity before the holy God, has observed,

> The old stance of the church that floats with a timeless, high impersonality — this is the very essence of the Christian God-relationship. This was before I was; this will be when I am gone. God's initiative toward me does not hang on the vagaries of my subjectivity. There is something in the old chants of the church that brought a necessary, audible balance to the self-incurvature of contemporary Christianity, and I very much lament its loss. . . .
>
> There is today a general religious bias toward a galloping subjectivity. But our first obligation to a text is to let it hang there

in celestial objectivity — not to ask what it means *to us*. A good
sermon or a good teaching job must begin with angelic objectivity.
There's something in the mood of our culture that hates that.
We want to hurry up and get to what something means to an
individual. But this notion presents a serious danger to the true
meaning of any important text — biblical, literary, or otherwise.
The text had a particular meaning before I saw it, and it will continue to mean that after I have seen it. It expresses an intention
that is meant to be heard by all, not interpreted according to any
one individual's preferences or biases.[13]

The rich and complex truths to which liturgy points come from beyond
the present. It was with such in mind that older works on liturgy such as
Luther Reed's *The Lutheran Liturgy* (1947, 1960) and Paul Zeller Stro-
dach's *A Manual on Worship* (1930, 1946) rightly stressed the objective
nature of liturgical worship in contrast to the subjective approach of
much non-liturgical worship.

Our notions of prayer and worship have shrivelled, and we have lost
the large understanding of prayer as an activity that includes private
as well as public devotion. We therefore attempt to cram it all into
public worship, and it cannot work. Subjectivity has its rightful place
primarily in the language and practice of private prayer. Objectivity has
its rightful place primarily in the language and practice of public prayer.
Both are necessary; each deprived of the other can be deadly.

Liturgical worship provides what we in the depth of our being need:
something external to us by which we can test ourselves, something beyond us by that we can shape our lives. Worship as it is enshrined in the
liturgy presents us with an objective reality which stands over against us
as judge, to challenge, to provoke, to entice us. Classic literature does
something of the same thing for us. Wendy Doniger has written of the
complexity of our relationship to the great imaginative achievements of
the past (among which the liturgy is surely to be numbered):

It may well be that it is the very *nature* of classics to be other,
to refer back to a lost golden age and to speak with an archaic
diction that we must strain to understand. This means that we
cannot possess our classics, if by "possess" we mean to internalize,
to comprehend completely, to experience as a non-other body of
literature.[14]

More succinctly, Harold Bloom, reviewing Alter and Kermode's *Literary Guide to the Bible*, wrote, "We do not contain the Bible, or Shakespeare, or Freud; they contain us."[15]

In a still larger sense, the church's liturgy challenges the self-centeredness of the human race by radically expanding our horizon. We humans, we are reminded, do not comprehend all life. Janet Lembke has written of "dangerous birds,"[16] dangerous because attending to them, watching them, learning their names and songs and ways, musing over them in the stillness of morning or in the quiet of dusk and finding the calmness of spirit it takes to really see them, changes the way we look at the world. Our very view of life shifts when we respond to the fascination of what C. S. Lewis called "other bloods." "We slip from our comfortably human-centered world into one in which we see that other living things, more ancient than we, get along perfectly well without us, a world in which we seem to be upstarts and intruders."[17]

In Daily Prayer the church on earth is reminded that it joins not only with the choirs of heaven in praising God but that it also joins the praise of the rest of creation, animate and inanimate, in their wordless praise of the Creator. Psalm 148, for example, invites praise from the heavens (sun, moon, stars, highest heaven, the waters above the heaven) and from the earth (sea monsters, the deep, fire, hail, snow, frost, stormy wind, mountains, trees, animals, human beings.) The great canticle *Benedicite omnia opera* is an elaboration of these invocations of the whole natural world to praise and magnify God forever.[18] In the Easter Vigil, the Lutheran text of the Exsultet, echoing ancient sources, commends the work of bees, who of their own substance have selflessly provided the wax from which was made the Easter candle, which is itself a model of self-giving for the good of others:

> We sing the glories
> of this pillar of fire,
> the brightness of which
> is not diminished,
> even when its light
> is divided and borrowed.

> For it is fed by the melting wax
> which the bees, your servants,
> have made for the substance
> of this candle.[19]

In the Eucharist, bread and wine are brought to the altar at the offering for use in the meal. In those gifts many commentators have found an expression of "a tripartite relationship of nature, humanity, and God in collaborative alliance."[20] The Creator has made a world that produces grain and grapes; these are then transformed by human agriculture and activity into bread and wine. Then the bread and wine are presented to God for further transformation or transsignification into the "bread of heaven" and the "cup of salvation," the body and blood of Christ. In the bread and wine that are presented in the offering is signified the long and necessary cooperation between humanity and nature. Fields are cleared, seeds cultivated over many centuries are planted, grain is harvested, milled, and baked. Vines are planted, pruned, and tended for years before a grape of quality can be gathered. The juice of the grape needs time to ferment and mature "before achieving the dignity of wine."[21] The elements of a common meal in many parts of the world — bread and wine — although they are themselves far from common or ordinary, become the elements of the Supper of the Lord, and the connection with the natural world is at least subtly maintained.

In the present Roman rite, the presider, lifting the presented bread from the altar says, "Blessed are you, Lord, God of all creation. Through your goodness we have this bread to offer, which earth has given and human hands have made. It will become for us the bread of life." Similarly, the presider takes the chalice with wine and water and says, "Blessed are you, Lord, God of all creation. Through your goodness we have this wine to offer, fruit of the vine and work of human hands. It will become our spiritual drink." Thus the wonder of life in the largest sense of the word is acknowledged and "the intimate union of cosmic energy and human industry in these simple gifts"[22] is recognized. Human labor has had an essential part to play in the production of the bread and wine, but the success of that labor depends in large and wondrous measure on the mysterious workings of life and growth. The world and life of nature are never far from the liturgy.

Submission to Conventions

Unless we understand the objective character of the liturgy we are liable to misuse and weaken its power to help us shape our lives. Mark Searle in a perceptive essay has pointed out that if liturgical language is the communication of information or the expression of private thoughts and feelings, then the presiding ministers will feel free to alter the texts to make them express more clearly what the presiding minister thinks or feels or believes that the community ought to feel or think. More-over, some may believe it necessary to manipulate the congregation so that it has the appropriate feelings as determined by the presider.[23] So a congregation is required to shout "Good morning!" to wake them up, to put them in a cheery, upbeat celebrative mood (even if for some it may be a rotten morning).

But liturgical language, as we have seen, is performative language; it accomplishes what it is spoken to achieve. And if that is so, then, as Searle argues, "I confess" is an act of confessing, not the externalization of imposed guilt feelings; "We believe in one God" is not a statement of an opinion or even a statement of one's own faith but an act of giving oneself to God and binding oneself to the faith of the church;[24] "Heaven and earth are full of your glory" is not a statement about the cosmos but an act of praise. Such acts may or may not be accompanied by appropriate feelings; what matters is that they are done.[25]

It is easy to see when feelings are absent in other people. A system-atic theologian took offense in his seminary chapel one morning when he noticed someone yawning while genuflecting at the words "and was made man" (*incarnatus est*) in the Nicene Creed; this afforded the theo-logian further confirmation of his belief that bodily gestures had little merit. It is not difficult to criticize such carelessness and a wandering mind, but, one wonders, why wasn't the theologian's mind on the text of the creed? His attention also was wandering, and without the bodily gesture to remind him of an appropriate attitude that he at that mo-ment did not feel. Just doing the form is not altogether bad. Luther himself, while commending "spiritual and sincere prayer," allowed that

> there is such a great measure of grace in the word of God that even a prayer that is spoken with the mouth and without devo-tion (with a sense of obedience) becomes fruitful and irritates the devil.[26]

Obedience stemming from a simple sense of duty, Luther says, is a mo-tive for "external prayer" that is not to be despised. In this, Luther was giving expression to a traditional view. Long before Luther, John Chrysostom advised his hearers, "And even if you do not understand the meaning of the words, for the time being teach your mouth to say them, for the tongue is sanctified by the words alone whenever it says them with good will."[27] The point, as Searle says, is attitude, not feelings. To mean what one says is to be willing to go along with what the words commit one to. The Holy Spirit calls and gathers the church, and once the community is gathered, the prayer that is offered is not one's own possession; indeed it is the Spirit who is praying within us.

Dietrich Bonhoeffer required his students at the seminary of the Confessing Church in Finkenwalde to read extended passages of the Bible and then to meditate and to pray on the basis of a brief text, often the same text for many consecutive days. He declared in *Life Together,* "The most promising method of prayer is to allow oneself to be guided by the word of the Scriptures, to pray on the basis of a word of Scripture. In this way we shall not become the victims of our own emptiness. Prayer means nothing else but the readiness and willingness to receive and appropriate the Word, and, what is more, to accept it in one's personal situation."[28] The Word of God shapes and informs our prayer, not our own emptiness. In Mark Searle's words,

> We are invited to lend ourselves to the prayer, rather than to pray out of our own meager resources. We are invited, not to express our feelings or thoughts, but to submit to the convention of this common prayer, to try it on, to adapt ourselves to its demands.... The prayers and texts of the liturgy invite us to assume the attitudes required by these conventional prayers; not to express feelings or thoughts we may not have, but to find ourselves within the words.[29]

As Cyprian admonished his hearers, "If we call God Father, we should act like God's children."[30] The church is the gathered people of God, the visible sign of the presence and action of Christ. The prayers of that assembly are therefore not our own but are given to us to appropriate, to make our own. We are to lose ourselves in Christ's prayer by allowing our immediate feelings to be swallowed up by his cosmic priesthood before the throne of the Holy One. The purpose of the liturgy is not to express our thoughts and feelings but to impress them, to shape and form them by shaping and forming our attitudes so that they conform to those of Christ. The congregation gathers to submit to the discipline of the rite, to learn from it, to grow into it and by it.

Anselm in his *Proslogion* captured in a memorable aphorism the appropriate stance of the church: faith seeking understanding.[31] The work of God (that is, our response of faith to the summons of the Holy Spirit) has priority; understanding follows. The Christian faith is known only from within the community of the church, as suggested by Philip's response to Nathanael's questioning, "Come and see" (John 1:46). The faith can be understood only from the inside by those who have made the prior commitment of faith, acceptance, belief. Those without a living and continuous relationship to the Christian community, who may drop in on a service of worship, should not expect or be expected to understand all that is going on. The Liturgy of St. John Chrysostom preserves a striking reminder of this relationship between the outsiders and the insiders. When the liturgy of the word is completed — the opening prayers, the reading of the Epistle and Gospel, the sermon, and the litany of the catechumens — which are open to all, the warning cry is raised by the priest, "The doors, the doors! All catechumens depart; let no catechumen remain." (No one ever leaves any more.) Then the offertory begins the liturgy for the initiated, the insiders. During the first five centuries of its life the church maintained the "discipline of the secret," the custom of concealing from the unbaptized its most sacred rites and doctrines. As anciently, so always: the mysteries of Christianity are most of all for the initiated, those who have committed themselves to follow the Way.

The psalms, which make up the core of Daily Prayer, have endured through the ages because generations upon generations have found in these ancient songs a window on the lives that God intends for his people. Luther said of the psalter,

> There you look into the hearts of all the saints.... The psalter holds you to the communion of saints and away from the sects. For it teaches you in joy, fear, hope, and sorrow to think and speak as all the saints have thought and spoken. In a word, if you would see the holy Christian church painted in living color and shape, comprehended in one little picture, then take up the psalter. There you have a fine, bright, pure mirror that will show you what Christendom is. Indeed you will find in it also yourself and the true *gnothi seauton* ("know thyself") as well as God himself and all creatures.[32]

In the psalms we can test ourselves against other, sometimes even alien, themes and ideas in order to foster our spiritual growth.

In private devotion as it was practiced some generations ago, the

daily memorization of a verse of Scripture encouraged those who pondered it throughout the day not only to make that verse their own but
also to give themselves to it, to shape and even transform their conduct
by it, to conform their lives to it. In many ways through the centuries
Christians have been moved and encouraged to imitate the lives of the
holy men and women who preceded them through the world, as together all of us are called to the imitation of Christ, "to conform our
lives to his," as a Lutheran postcommunion prayer puts it.[33]

Luther calls the psalter a mirror that shows what Christianity is.
The liturgy too is such a mirror, not a mere looking glass that only
reflects and gives back what we already know, encouraging our deadly
self-incurvature, but a mirror that tells the truth about us and reveals
accurately who we really are. Such a mirror was the *Mirror for Magis-
trates*, a collection of stories in verse by several poets, begun in 1563,
concerning the misfortunes of the great figures of English history as
a warning to those presently in power. In John Doberstein's *Minister's Prayer Book* the anthology for each day concludes with a passage
from Max Lackmann called "A Mirror for Ministers" (*Beichtspiegel fuer
Pfarrer*) providing searching questions by which ministers may examine
their lives and ministry to reveal their shortcomings and failures and
to encourage renewed dedication and faithfulness.[34] Hans Asmussen,
in another passage included in Doberstein's book, provides another
confession-mirror to assist ministers in applying the Law to their own
lives to show where they have not measured up.[35]

Such mirrors show us what we by ourselves may be unable to see;
and sometimes they may show us what we do not want to see, what we
are unwilling to admit. Thus the liturgy reveals what we really are —
hard, angry, bitter, perhaps — as a corrective to what we think we
are — pleasant, happy, contented. Such use of a mirror is the work
of the Law. But the mirror of the liturgy can also present us with the
Gospel, a mirror by which we can see not just our unpleasant, sinful
selves looking back disconcertingly at us but in which we can discern
the lineaments of the image that God has of us. Such a mirror provides a portrayal of God's knowledge of what we can become, a picture
of the stature into which we are to grow (2 Cor. 3:18). So the liturgy
forms and shapes and develops our understanding of the faith and of
our share in it.

The purpose of the liturgy is not to express our thoughts and feelings
but to develop them, and like any good school the liturgy expands our

horizon, liberating us from captivity to the moment and to the familiar. Expansion of horizons is always both terrifying and exhilarating. The liturgy as it teaches us breaks down barriers and uproots the hedges that wall us in and confine us to our comfortable and familiar little world. It tears open the curtains that conceal what lies beyond and opens new vistas, enlarging the scope of our sight and imagination, encouraging us to move out and explore new territory and new ideas. Because the liturgy does not always express what we think or feel it has the potential to transform those who share in it.

The liturgy of the church provides us with a grand complexity, wonderful in its richness. Our reaction and response will vary from week to week, year to year. Like any work of art, as Nelson Goodman observes, the liturgy "may be successively, offensive, fascinating, comfortable, and boring," for such are the vicissitudes of knowledge. The peak of interest in a symbol, he suggests, may occur somewhere midway in the passage from the obscure to the obvious,[36] and this may occur at different times for different individuals.

> But there is endurance and renewal, too. Discoveries become available knowledge only when preserved in accessible form; the trenchant and laden symbol does not become worthless when it becomes familiar, but is incorporated in the base for further exploration. And where there is density in the symbol system, familiarity is never complete and final; another look may always disclose significant new subtleties. Moreover, what we read from and learn through a symbol varies with what we bring to it. Not only do we discover the world through our symbols, but we understand and reappraise our symbols progressively in the light of our growing experience.[37]

A symbol that may bore us by its familiarity can when heard in a new context of history or of one's individual life take on surprising, challenging, consoling new life and be reappropriated by those who had become accustomed to its use. Portrayals of the resurrection or Holy Baptism, for example, take on powerful meaning when seen and felt following the death of a loved one. Between World War I and World War II German theologians became convinced that the figure of the devil was no longer tolerable for sophisticated modern people and found North American theologians hopelessly laggard in maintaining their belief in the existence of such a figure. After World War II American theologians had caught up with European liberalism and had discarded the devil. The Europeans were astonished again. Having seen and participated in the brutality of Nazism, the devastation of the war, and the Holocaust, they found the old symbol of unfathomable evil absolutely essential. Perhaps there is nothing in the church's treasury that is entirely and permanently obsolete.

The liturgy is a treasury of discoveries expressed through symbols and discoveries enabled by symbols, and that vast treasury represents a millennia-long process of growth and learning and appropriation and expression. Not every symbol and image is of equal intensity, and when a successful image becomes familiar it often slides for a time into the benign twilight of an undemanding cliché shorn of novelty and surprise. Cliché is usually condemned by writers and teachers of writing; Donald Hall calls clichés dull cinderblocks that prevent thinking, "reprocessed garbage."[38] Instead, he commends Confucius's advice, "Make it new."[39] For individual exploration and expression such advice is surely helpful. But Michael Frayn in his collection of aphorisms, *Constructions*, has taken a second look at the despised cliché:

> The more one thinks about our common kit of metaphors for mental states and events, the less inclined one is to take it for granted, or dismiss it as banal. "At the back of one's mind," "to run over the alternatives," "to reach a decision," "something stirred in her memory," "he groped for words" — they're brilliant! A whole literature, really, trodden down into the soil like last year's leaves, fertilizing, unrecognized and forgotten, whatever pushes above the ground now.[40]

Hall's "garbage" becomes Frayn's "fertilizer," not rubbish to be discarded in some landfill or dumped out of sight at sea but an organic compost of rich nutrients that continues to nourish the growth of language. The language of liturgy, like the language of theology, is full of terms and phrases that may have lost their original potency but that are not therefore to be discarded. They can serve to suggest and nurture new variants of old themes. Similarly, the complexity of the liturgy, filtered and digested through the centuries, is a powerful residue still abundant with latent energy and the delight of discovery for those who learn to attend to it.

Images of the church as family or a community of friends can be helpful, but a more adequate image for our time may be the church as city.[41] St. Augustine had it right, centuries ago: the church is the City of God. He learned it from the New Testament. The writer to the Hebrews says of the nomad Abraham, his family, and descendents that while in the promised land they lived in tents "as in a foreign land." Even the land of promise was not their permanent home, for they looked in hopeful expectation to a substantial and permanent place, not the tents of nomads. "They looked forward to the city that has foundations, whose architect and builder is God" (Heb. 11:9–10). Even in the land that had been allotted to them by divine decree they lived as strangers and foreigners in search of a homeland, for their real and abiding home lay still in the future. God, whose plans in time are perpetually unfinished, who is forever driving on, had a still better place prepared — a city, the heavenly Jerusalem (Rev. 22:21), the mother of us all (Gal. 4:26). Such an image of the city not only gives hope for the future, bright with promise. It points to the vocation of the church to include and redeem all the dimensions of society. It captures the richness of the centuries of discovery and construction and renovation, and it looks toward the promised New Jerusalem, that image of redeemed society with its cosmic symbolism, its grandeur, glory, and majesty.

The liturgy of the church, its best school, provides the church with a vision of the community and the city as they might and should be, of the wonders that lie behind an otherwise opaque reality, of the goal toward which all creation moves, providing "a foretaste of the feast to come"[42] — the messianic banquet celebrated in a temple not made with hands and set forever in holy Zion, the city of the living God.

Chapter Seven

BEYOND THE BOUNDARIES

A s SAMUEL JOHNSON REMARKED when he began work on the *Dictionary* that made him famous, any living language is constantly changing.[1] Style, grammatical patterns, vocabulary are never static, for language is influenced by the attitudes, beliefs, and customs of a people. As the Christian community encounters new experiences and new situations it continuously fashions new patterns of speaking and acting, and the new is assimilated with the old in ever larger, ever expanding unities. Centuries of assimilation and reinterpretation give a rich texture of meaning to the liturgy. Particular phrases and larger units and actions resonate on several different levels, appealing to a diverse congregation in a variety of ways.

Deepened Sensitivity

In the last decades of the twentieth century careful users of language increasingly learned to be sensitive to certain implications of the language they use. Most try to avoid gender-specific language when speaking of humanity in general and to avoid words and phrases that, however subtly, may diminish the worth of one group, whether based on gender or race or age.[2] Much of this was found relatively easy to accomplish once one became convinced of its necessity — avoiding "man" and its variants and compounds as a generic term, avoiding stereotypes and negative connotations of "black," "Indian," and such. Revisers of liturgical language shared these concerns, which have the support of most of the academic community and much of the press and other media.[3] To allow, for example, the exclusive and excessive masculinity of Henry Van Dyke's lines in his hymn "Joyful, Joyful, We Adore Thee"

> Father love is reigning o'er us,
> Brother love binds man to man[4]

108

or the racism lurking in lines in Robert Campbell's translation of a seventeenth-century Latin office hymn

> Where the paschal blood is poured
> Death's dark angel sheathes his sword[5]

was, at least to many, no longer tolerable.[6]

Nonetheless, well-intentioned efforts to eliminate bias from our language can be deceptive. Donald Hall has given the wise counsel that "we will never destroy bias, but we can learn to see bias."[7] We cannot eradicate it, for such peculiar perspective seems built into human nature and probably cannot be eliminated this side of the consummation. We can accept bias as a fact although we do not approve of it; we cannot get rid of it, but we can learn to recognize it. Indeed, given the ineradicable character of bias, recognition of it is perhaps more useful in the long run than efforts to get rid of it. If bias is bound to appear in one form or another, we would do better to recognize it for what it is and then deal with it than to eliminate every word and phrase that we think reveals bias and then assume that the problem has been taken care of. Out of sight does not guarantee out of mind.

Bias is easily recognizable in others, as Hall notes, but it is much more difficult to recognize in ourselves. Considerable humility is required, and that is not at all easy to achieve. Merely following guidelines for linguistic use or tinkering with (or, for that matter, radically altering) the language of the liturgy may lead us to deceive ourselves into the confidence that *we* are now free of prejudice.

Avoiding bias is an exceedingly complex and delicate matter. In an effort to avoid bias it does no good to replace one stereotype with another, replacing, for example, images of the strong masculine father with images of the tender feminine mother. Not all men are strong, not all women are tender, and the admirable person may be one in whom toughness and tenderness are mixed. Indeed, the biblical picture of God is exactly that. The replacement of masculine imagery with feminine may not only be no gain; it can in fact be a serious deformation that severs connection with tradition and separates one from the roots of the faith, replacing one error with another still more dangerous because it may be less obvious.

An instructive example of the pervasive complexity of bias is the case of Bartolomé de Las Casas (1474–1566), who is commemorated on the Lutheran calendar on July 17. A staunch defender of the indigenous peoples of Central America and the (West) Indies, he for a time suggested that Indian slaves be replaced by Africans, who were, he thought, demonstrably better suited to heavy labor in hot climates. Openness in one area did not prevent his blindness in another. To his credit, it needs to be noted, Las Casas outgrew that reprehensible notion and came to protest the enslavement of Africans as well as Indians.

Still more difficult, from the present perspective at least, is what is often called "naming God," for the imagery and titles associated with the deity not only have been hallowed by centuries, even millennia, of use but are often drawn from the Bible itself, which is received by Jews and Christians alike as the definitive and normative record of the revelation of God. The name of the Holy Trinity, for example, in its classic formulation wrought through centuries of struggle and even warfare is "Father, Son, and Holy Spirit." This heavily weighted masculine language with reference to God, who is beyond gender, may seem undesirable and in need of reformulation. But it is not a simple matter of changing the offending words. The current controversy over naming God is in fact a struggle for Christian identity. The name of the Holy Trinity above all is critical, for through the centuries the Holy Trinity has been the test of orthodoxy.[8] Our choice of words for God has been shaped by God's choice of the historical moment and means of incarnation, and the continuing task of the church is to be faithful to what it receives as the normative record of revelation, the Holy Scripture. Father, Son, and Holy Spirit derives from the Bible as the name for God that has been provided by Christ's history.

In the world of the Bible changing a name is never without profound and revolutionary significance. A person with a new name is nothing less than a new person. Jacob, the fugitive of dubious character, becomes Israel, the one who strives with God and in whom and for whom God strives. Saul, the most violent persecutor of Christians, becomes their foremost missionary known by his Roman name, Paul. In the Roman Church still, when a man is elected pope, he chooses a new name by which he will be known in his papacy. The cardinal archbishop of Milan, Giovanni Battista Montini, upon election as bishop of Rome became known as Paul VI, a name chosen in part because of its ecumenical significance and appeal. But, except for the papacy and some who enter religious orders, in the modern world names usually have less significance. They are thought of as merely arbitrary labels by which we distinguish and refer to things and people. We call a child

"Sarah," princess, a pleasant thought but not necessarily a royal reality. In the world of the ancient Semites, however, name and reality were interrelated. The introduction to the Babylonian creation poem *Enuma Elish* describes the conditions before the creation; the Akkadian text describes how things were before they were named. Name and existence belong together, as is made clear in the opening chapters of the Bible. The Creator speaks a name and what was named springs into being. Humans give names and order, categorizing and defining the complexity of creation into recognizable quantities. The naming of the animals perfects creation.[9] Name is related to reality, and name is related to personality. A name expresses the essence of a person, and a change in name indicates a change in character. In the biblical tradition, changing God's biblically authorized name comes dangerously close to the unthinkable: changing God.

The substitutions for the traditional triune name that have been suggested so far are unsatisfactory, verging on heresy (specifically, modalism, as in "Creator, Redeemer, Sanctifier") and requiring more explication than the traditional formulation (as in "Lover, Beloved, Mutual Friend"). It is not, however, simply a matter of waiting through experimentation until someone comes up with a substitute formula and language that will satisfy most people. The problem lies, as Christopher Seitz argues in an incisive and important essay, "not with our texts, but with our own fast-diminishing 'reader competence' as a church and as a culture for comprehending the subtle world of biblical discourse."[10] The essential point, difficult but surely not impossible for modern people to comprehend, is that the Bible uses masculine language for God while at the same time insisting that God is "neither male nor female." The Bible clearly and consistently rejects human sexuality as the chief means of comprehending the divine. God, to whom the Bible consistently refers with masculine pronouns, is beyond human sexual categories. The creator God is the wholly other, Lord of all creation who is not to be constrained by any image.

In Judaism such was the fear of compromising the absolute otherness of God that not only were representations of God forbidden but also representations of humans and animals, and the adornment of synagogues consists traditionally of geometric patterns and designs. The powerful presence of the First Commandment (the second in Protestant numbering) looms over discussions of the name of God: "You shall not make for yourself an idol, whether in the form of anything that is

in heaven above, or that is on the earth beneath, or that is in the water under the earth. You shall not bow down to them or worship them:
for I the Lord your God am a jealous God" (Exod. 20:4–5). An idol,
as the prophets make clear, is an impossible thing, a god made by mortals, a god made in our own image and likeness to meet our assumed
needs and desires, to be what we want God to be. Idolatry turns creation upside down. Mortals become the creator, and their god becomes
the created creature. Such an idol made by human hands and skill is
entirely unworthy of worship and is properly the subject of ridicule, as
in Isaiah's satires (7:7–8 and 44:9–20). Luther commented on the First
Commandment, "in order to show that God will not have this commandment taken lightly but will strictly watch over it, he has attached
to it, first, a terrible threat and, then, a beautiful, comforting promise."[11]

The grammatical gender of Israel's God has a variety of causes, many
now lost to us. Patriarchy had a role, as did Israel's struggle with the
goddesses of the surrounding patriarchal societies. But Holy Scripture
confronts us with a profound and compelling paradox. God is called Father and is referred to with masculine pronouns in a system that insists
that God is not a man, not male. God is the wholly Other, and yet is
addressed in personal terms. Thus God is and is not Father: Father as
in the intimate personal, familial relationship, but a heavenly Father,
beyond all human parenting, who is none other than the Holy One of
Israel, the Most High. The sources of patriarchy are to be sought elsewhere than in the biblical language and imagery. Our ancestors who
inhabited the world of the Bible, Seitz argues, did not confuse human
fathers with representations of God as a Father, encouraging men to
feel the honor of inclusion and women the shame of exclusion. Men as
well as women knew and felt the great gulf between God and humanity,
unbridgeable from our side, the radical distinction between Creator and
creatures, and were grateful that God could deliver his people in ways
that mortals — men as well as women — could never do. The otherness even of the God who is described with masculine pronouns stands
as judge over all human striving and desires and sin. Oppressive males
and submissive females stand alike under the same Judge, "our Father
in heaven."

What gives pause to many who resist changing the name and pronouns for God is the very modernity of the present questions. By
focusing on the gender of the pronouns and the massive (but not exclusively) masculine terminology, Seitz and Brevard Childs[12] insist, the

paradox is irreparably damaged, the heavenly Father's transcendence of gender is broken, and human sexuality becomes a principal means of comprehending God. We have lost the biblical world as a key agent in informing our world in the present age, and have in Seitz's words, lost "confidence in how to read and live into these biblical stories, from the Old and New Testament." Seitz sets the issue squarely: "masculine language for God functioned within a specific biblical realm that every reader knew was distinct and set over against the daily best efforts of men and women." What modern readers of the Bible and modern worshippers must struggle against is the loss of the biblical world "as a trustworthy, challenging, cleansing world." Seitz concludes,

> The chief task before the church is not to sanitize and correct the Bible from the outside, but rather to learn again from the inside the connected universe of the Bible's presentation; to learn to become competent readers again of a scripture whose intention is not only to include but to address and judge and cleanse and save.

It is the same point made throughout this book. The language of the liturgy, immersed as it is in the language and thought of the Bible, requires us to learn the language, new to us, of symbolism and ritual. The principal problems lie not with the imagery but with the competence of the readers of the Bible and the doers of the liturgy to experience themselves and their world in terms of the story of Israel and of Jesus.[13] A religion worth one's time is not an expression or projection of oneself or one's own idea of the world but rather an external world that shapes and forms believers in its image, which is grander than any individual can imagine or comprehend.

The contingency of "proper" names has been recognized by modern students of language, literature, and culture. Lévi-Strauss and particularly Jacques Derrida in *De la grammatologie* have shown that "proper" names function as a systematizing, classificatory principle rather than constituting adequate appellation that coincides perfectly with a signified or referent.[14] More simply put, metaphorical statements "always contain a whisper, 'It is and it is not.' "[15] The divine name above all is a manifestation of God's presence, and the disclosure of the Name of God is particularly precious. Pious Jews did not pronounce the Tetragrammaton YHWH, and Christians at the name of the Holy Trinity would bow their heads or make the sign of the cross. Yet even the divine Name must of necessity fail to express adequately the being and character of

God. The doctrine and the Name of the most Holy Trinity brings us
to the boundary of human conception and imagination. God is (and is
not) Father, Son, and Holy Spirit.

Liturgical Language

In the struggle to "purify the dialect of the tribe"[16] no doubt some of
what is resisted today will be seen by future generations as the obvi-
ously correct path. Luther Reed, late in his long life, in an otherwise
insightful essay,[17] defended the use of King James English in the liturgy
by asking rhetorically, "Would you like to see and sing 'We praise you.
We bless you. We worship you. We glorify you' or, at the end of all
prayers, 'through our Lord Jesus Christ, your Son, who lives and reigns
with You'?" By the last quarter of the twentieth century it was obvious
that nearly all of English-speaking Christianity had answered his question with a resounding "Yes." Nonetheless (things are seldom as simple
as they seem) one might observe, "thee" is a much more pleasing sound
than "you," which has about it an ominous echo. In a passage in *The
Pilgrim's Progress* John Bunyan by the "oo" sound suggests the fear and
trembling of the two children of the spies who are fleeing for their lives
from the Shadow of Death as they warn Christian, "Back, back; and
would have you to do so too, if either life or peace is prized by you."[18]

What is resisted today may in time become clearly desirable. On
the other hand, revision must preserve the authentic tradition against
that innovation which would distort or destroy it. The choice is seldom
clear from a close perspective. Moreover, the distressing fact is that all
too often in religious and liturgical history, progress toward adaptation
has come at the expense of the imagination,[19] and the people are the
poorer for it.

The old and the familiar, even that which seems at first sight obsolete, is not necessarily a candidate for retirement. Respect for liturgy
and tradition (and Scripture too) encourages a second look, a reinterpretation, a reappropriation in ways suitable to contemporary contexts.
What can "Father" mean to an abused or abandoned family? some ask
with a newly discovered sensitivity. Yet others testify that the image is
precious; it can represent the father that the abused family wishes that
it had. And surely, abuse is not new in the late twentieth century, nor,
for that matter, is it limited to fathers. What can the picture of the

Good Shepherd mean to people in the ghettoes and barrios of modern cities? In fact, most people, wherever they live, have never seen a shepherd, and those sheep-herders who do exist in modern society ride the range in pick-up trucks. Yet the Good Shepherd has proved to be a surprisingly durable image, still a popular dedication for churches even in urban areas and an inspiration for many related church dedications, particularly in Lutheran circles, such as Shepherd of the Hills, Shepherd of the Valley, Shepherd of the Bay; and clergy are still called "pastor."

"King" as a title for God and for Christ, one supposes, can mean little to a world in which there are few absolute monarchs left and none in any country that we can easily identify. Yet even such an apparently obsolete term can be useful in relativizing worldly power and teaching that no earthly monarch is absolute. Only Jesus Christ has the right and authority to be King and Lord of the nations. All human authority is ultimately subservient to the one Sovereign. The creation of contemporary pictures of God and Christ to replace monarchical ones can easily border on the banal or the comical as in Christ the President, for the church is not a democracy nor is it a publicly owned corporation. One must not sell short the ability of congregations to move beneath the surface irrelevancies to embrace the deeper and enduring truths to which an apparently obsolete image gives focus.

The way ahead, therefore, at least to those who have such a deep regard for the accumulated experience of the ages, commonly called tradition, that they can neither abandon nor deform nor deface it, is not to jettison inherited language and figures and metaphors but judiciously to supplement them with newer insights. In this way the new attempts can be tested, examined, and judged, for we cannot at short sight know what will take hold and endure to the benefit of future generations. It is not that new attempts must only support and supplement old ideas and images. They may indeed challenge and even at times contradict them. Stephen Prickett notes that translation, where there is no effective equivalent, is one of the major sources of change and enrichment of a living language.[20] A language develops in range and subtlety of expression *not* by means of receptivity to translation, but through its *resistance* to new words and concepts. It is not equivalences but *dissimilarities* that force the modification and change necessary to accommodate new associative patterns of thought. The liturgy is large enough and strong enough to support contradictory ideas as a way of expanding our ability to conceive of and express the fullness of our experience. There is risk involved, to be sure, for as my teacher Morse Peckham was fond of observing, there is a Gresham's Law of language as well as of money: bad language drives out good. But nonetheless it is a risk worth taking as language changes and grows and develops.

In all this, the goal in the expression of liturgical worship is language that is (1) heightened, not the language of everyday, for the ideas it expresses are not everyday; (2) cultic, indeed secret, for although it may be overheard by those outside, the language is addressed primarily to those inside the church and is expressive of their faith and commitment, rather than to outsiders with a view to their conversion; (3) evocative, not primarily didactic and instructional; (4) honest, not asserting more (or less) than Christianity relying on Scripture can be sure of.

Out of frustration with the magnitude of the task, the lament is heard, "We need a Cranmer."[21] We need the genius of the creator of the 1549 *Book of Common Prayer.* But the real need is not for a towering figure with considerable literary, theological, and political skills. The sixteenth century was the beginning of a great age of English literature that produced not only Shakespeare and a vast number of other notable writers of considerable power but a whole society that delighted in the use of the language in which nearly everyone, from Queen Elizabeth down, not only wrote poetry but wrote poetry of enviable quality.

There is little reason to be optimistic. "We are the prisoners of an age which is at best unimaginative," declared the English priest and poet R. S. Thomas.[22]

> The task may well seem hopeless when the poet is confronted by this Augean stable — the gobbledygook of technologists and critics, the pompous yet repellently servile idiom of business correspondence, the reach-me-down, utility style of most newspapers, the weird jargon concocted by civil servants, and worst of all, the hectic flush imparted to language by publicists and advertisers. The bogus floweriness of the latter, the barbarous, pretentious, or complacently drab tones of the others, are enough to make poetry despair. Poetry's language should be a heightening of the common language; but, when so much of that language is either vile or without flavour, the poet has no sound basis from which to work.[23]

C. Day Lewis, like so many others, places the blame largely upon advertising, for, he observes, if one "speaks eloquently, with panache,"[24] we suspect insincerity: that person wants something from us. Peter R. Pouncey, when he was president of Amherst College, in evidence that "as a nation we seem to be getting worse at using words" cited the examples of battlefield letters home from soldiers in the Civil War and from more recent wars, from common soldiers as well as officers. He found "a sad deterioration in the strength and vividness of the prose" and concluded that "overall Civil War soldiers wrote better than our contemporaries, and I find it hard to avoid concluding that they thought better as well."[25] As always, writing and thinking go together. The need is not for a lone Cranmer to solve our linguistic, aesthetic, and theological problems but rather for a society that can think and write with such depth and sensitivity as to give rise to and support such a reformer.

One example may show the flattening of language and imagination that has taken place over the past few centuries. Augustus Montague Toplady's vivid final stanza of his beloved hymn "Rock of Ages, Cleft for Me" was originally

> Whilst I draw this fleeting breath,
> When my eyestrings break in death,
> When I soar through tracts unknown,
> See thee on thy judgment throne,
> Rock of Ages, cleft for me,
> Let me hide myself in thee.

It was tamed to

> While I draw this fleeting breath,
> When my eyelids close in death....

In other hymnals it was made still flatter,

> When my eyes are closed in death....

Bland and colorless stretches abound in language that is smoothed out so as not to be embarrassing or offensive. The history of the rewriting of hymns is too often the story through several centuries of a general flattening of language as one generation found the vigorous phrases of an earlier day too strong for its taste. Some troublesome stanzas were omitted, others rewritten, often yielding comatose results.[26]

When language shrivels, those who use (and misuse) it shrivel also, and the impoverishment and corruption of language is felt as a loss of

power and a personal sense of impotence, a narrowing of consciousness, and confinement to an inarticulate dumbness. The revision of
liturgical language is no trivial task, for language, as George Steiner
reminds us, "seeks vengeance on those who cripple it."[27] The trivializa-
tion, coarsening, and deformation of liturgical language impoverishes
its users spiritually and theologically. Giving attention to the reformation of language of the liturgy therefore means giving attention to
the fundamental nature of Christianity. It is not a task for a solitary
individual, no matter how talented. It is a task to be accomplished
through the nurture and development of a Christian people who can
use the liturgy with sensitivity and perception and find in it a powerful means of spiritual formation, allowing it to work in them and
on them.

T. S. Eliot, writing of the poetry of George Herbert as well as all
poetry, noted that

> enjoyment is the beginning as well as the end. We must enjoy the
> poetry before we attempt to penetrate the poet's mind; we must
> enjoy it before we understand it, if the attempt to understand it
> is to be worth the trouble.[28]

It is a useful reminder for those who would revise the liturgy. The beginning is enjoyment and the end is a deep and abiding joy, a happiness
usually translated "blessedness." Ultimately, the liturgy, like a poem in
Archibald MacLeish's definition, "should not mean but be."[29] The goal
is not to mean something else, as if the primary job was to get away
from the text as quickly as possible, but confidently and simply to be
what it is — a many-layered, symbol-laden dramatic expression that can
appeal to us on many levels at once and in many dimensions.

On the Frontier

Temples are always liminal.[30] They represent a decisive moment of
crossing, a confrontation with the other side. Such holy places built
on the border invite us to pass over their thresholds from the familiar to the unfamiliar, from the comfortable to the disturbing, from this
world to the next. In these temples worshippers not only see holy objects set before them for contemplation but they hear holy words and
participate in holy actions; and the temple, never complete in itself,

remains a threshold of a something more, impelling those who enter it to a transformed way of living. The medieval cathedrals and their modern imitators like the Cathedral Church of St. John the Divine in New York City were deliberately left unfinished. Niches were left unfilled with statues of saints, blocks of stone were left uncarved. The point was that the vigor of the faith continues unabated and that there is room for more in the great choirs of the blessed; there is in fact a place for us as well as for those who come after us.

A notable feature of Byzantine church architecture is the iconostasis that stands between the congregation and the altar area. As early as 317, with the construction of one of the earliest chancel barriers at Tyre, the sanctuary is described as the "holy of holies."[31] The theme has continued throughout Byzantine liturgical writing. Absolute mystery, the radically transcendent ground of existence, has become incarnate in Christ, but the absolute mystery continues to be wholly other. The iconostasis is an architectural demonstration of this insight. Moreover, the strong sense of eschatology is another reason why a clearly marked holy space is desirable in Byzantine churches. The eschatological fulfillment is understood in the Christian East as "the definitive revelation and participation in God as absolute, infinite, All-fulfilling Holiness,"[32] and so a visible holy place makes this promise and expectation vivid. Yet again, the holy of holies reinforces the understanding that the church and the liturgy are not self-contained realities. The church is more than the present gathered community. The liturgy celebrated around the earth participates in a transcendent liturgy. This is a characteristic Eastern insight. St. Vladimir's representatives who had travelled to Constantinople in their search for an appropriate religion for the emerging Russia came back with their cry of wonder, "We did not know whether we were in heaven or on earth!" The goal of Christian pilgrims is the heavenly Jerusalem and the liturgy of Christ before the throne of the Father revealed in the Eucharist. The sanctuary (that is, the holy place) as a witness to the eschaton "relativizes all places, a piece of this earth which relativizes the importance of this earth. Such contrasts enable us to see the world in proper perspective."[33] The presence of the clearly delineated holy place encourages the congregation to develop a forward and transcendent orientation, going beyond itself "because what it views during the liturgy is beyond itself."[34]

In Byzantine churches the abundance of iconography is dazzling in keeping with the prolixity of Byzantine worship generally. Patriarch

Photius (died ca. 895) gives an insight into the Byzantine penchant for abundant decoration:

> It is as if one had entered heaven itself with no one barring the way from any side, and was illuminated by the beauty in all forms shining all around like so many stars, so is one utterly amazed. Thenceforth it seems that everything is in ecstatic motion, and the church itself is circling round. For the spectator, through his whirling about in all directions and being constantly astir, which he is forced to experience by the variegated spectacle on all sides, imagines that his personal condition is transferred to the object.[35]

The appointments of the church building engender ecstasy and subsequently cause the beholder to perceive ecstasy within the appointments. Modern people close their eyes to gain concentration in prayer; Byzantine worshippers open their eyes and stare with fixed gaze until their souls are shaken in their depths.[36]

The liturgy done in these liminal temples, like the temples themselves, brings us to the frontier, the far boundary of articulateness and imagination. But there is not an end to the journey. As long as the world lasts, work remains to be done. Christians live on the border between this world and the next, living now in the not yet.

Christian temples are places in which powerfully energetic words are uttered and heard, and those life-giving words make all the difference. A visible object, Northrop Frye observes, brings one to a respectful halt in front of it, but the word listened to and acted upon is the starting point of a course of action.[37] A liturgical procession begins not with the sight of the processional cross moving into position but with a verbal command,

> Let us go forth in peace.
> *In the name of Christ. Amen.*

So it is always in the places where Christians gather to do their liturgy. Signs of enduring reality, the gathering places can themselves never be more than places of temporary repose. The richness and abundance of the objects used as foci in Christian worship may for a time bring us to a pause before them as the procession makes its station. In our symbolic journey around the church building as in our life-long journey through this world toward the next we pause for contemplation and prayer before an altar, a statue, an icon, a cross, a bank of candles, a painting or sculpture, a window. But the still more profound depths of the word and the signs of the liturgy and their interaction, like the music of worship, urge us to keep moving and impel us to deeds beyond the temple because of what we have seen and heard and tasted in that beloved place of refreshment.

We respond to the Gospel invitation, "Come and see," and we give ourselves to the work of the church's prayer. Then, this having been done, in its rhythm of gathering and scattering, the assembly disperses to its tasks in the world. They assemble to give and receive divine service, and they disperse to extend divine service to those in need. Their knowledge of the world's needs is ever deepened by the work of praise and prayer to which they give themselves, and their praise and prayer are ever deepened by the work they do in the world. So it must be until the end of time. The Christian liturgy, in a reaffirmation of the ancient understanding of the creative energy of words to make and to move and to accomplish, issues in a clear and compelling ethical directive that can be understood in its depth only by those who have been taught, informed, and shaped by the weekly gathering around the font and the book and the table: "Go in peace. Serve the Lord."

NOTES

Preface

1. Gregory Dix, *The Shape of the Liturgy* (New York: Seabury Press, 1982), 369.

2. Quoted in Vilmos Vajta, *Luther on Worship* (Philadelphia: Muhlenberg Press, 1958), 20.

3. See Günther Stiller, *Johann Sebastian Bach and Liturgical Life in Leipzig,* trans. Herbert J. A. Bouman, Daniel F. Poellot, Hilton C. Oswald; ed. Robin A. Leaver (St. Louis: Concordia Publishing House, 1984).

4. Quoted by G. H. Bantock, "The Social and Intellectual Background," *The New Pelican Guide to English Literature,* ed. Boris Ford, vol. 7, *From James to Eliot* (New York: Penguin, 1983), 50.

Chapter One – The Language of the Liturgy

1. The Second Helvetic Confession (written 1562, first published 1566) 23.1: "Licet sane privatim precari quavis lingua quam quis intelligat, sed publicae preces in sacris coetibus vulgari lingua vel omnibus cognita fieri debent." Given in *The Creeds of Christendom,* ed. Philip Schaff (New York: Harper and Bros., 1877), 3:296.

2. For example, in "Conversations on the Craft of Poetry," a tape supplement to Cleanth Brooks and Robert Penn Warren's *Understanding Poetry* (3d ed., 1959): "I like to say, guardedly, that I could define poetry this way: It is that which is lost out of both prose and verse in translation." Given in Elaine Barry, *Robert Frost on Writing* (New Brunswick, N.J.: Rutgers University Press, 1973), 159. Philip Dormer Stanhope, the Fourth Earl of Chesterfield (1694–1773) declared that "nothing improves in translation except a bishop."

3. Luther D. Reed, *The Lutheran Liturgy* rev. ed. (Philadelphia: Muhlenberg Press, 1960), 481. The Latin collect that Dr. Horn praised was "Vota quaesumus domine supplicantis populi caelesti pietate prosequere, ut et quae agenda sunt videant, et ad implenda quae viderint convalescant. Per dominum." It is to be noted that Horn was able to assume that in the Lutheran Church at least the clergy in the early years of the twentieth century would sometimes say their prayers in Latin.

4. "Omnipotens sempiterne deus qui celesti simul et terrena moderaris, supplicationes populi tui clementer exaudi, et pacem tuam nostris concede temporibus. Per dominum." The collect was assigned to the Second Sunday after the Epiphany in previous Roman, Lutheran, and Anglican books.

5. *Second Progress Report of the Revision of the Roman Missal* (Washington, D.C.: International Commission on English in the Liturgy, 1990), 28.

6. Eric Fromm, *The Forgotten Language* (New York: Grove Press, 1957), vi. In a widely quoted remark, the Roman Catholic liturgist Romano Guardini, in a letter to Msgr. Johannes Wagner, April 1, 1964, observed with regard to the liturgy that what was required of modern people was to "relearn a forgotten way of doing things and recapture lost attitudes" (*Herder Correspondence*, August 1964, 237–39).

7. This oft-quoted tag apparently derives from an essay by John L. Lowes, "The Noblest Monument of English Prose" in the *Harvard Alumni Bulletin* and reprinted in his *Essays in Appreciation* (New York: Houghton Mifflin Co., 1936), 3–31. The phrase was denounced by T. S. Eliot in his essay "Religion and Literature" (1935); the Harvard alumnus had apparently seen and disliked the original essay.

8. Ian A. Gordon, *The Movement of English Prose* (Bloomington: Indiana University Press, 1966), 100. See also T. R. Henn, *The Bible as Literature* (New York: Oxford University Press, 1970), 46–47, 50–51; see also C. S. Lewis, *The Literary Impact of the Authorized Version* (London: Athlone Press, 1950), repr. in Lewis, *They Asked for a Paper* (London: Geoffrey Bles, 1962).

9. Henn, *The Bible as Literature*, 47, comments on the translation of 1 Kings 19:12 that Coverdale's "a styll soft hyssinge" became in the Matthew Bible "a small, still voice" and in the Authorized Version the familiar "a still small voice" thus achieving "a final harmony on the vowels *i–a–oi*. It is this subtlety of cadence which appears to give the impression of the thing perfectly and finally said."

10. Luther D. Reed, "A Pan-Lutheran Liturgy and Hymnal," *Response* VII, 4 (Easter, 1966), 207.

11. *The Anglican Service Book,* a Traditional Language Adaptation of the Book of Common Prayer prepared by the Church of the Good Shepherd, Rosemont, Pennsylvania (1992), claims to be preserving "the traditional language of Anglican worship."

12. Walter Howard Frere, *A Collection of His Papers on Historical Subjects,* ed. J. H. Arnold and E. G. P. Wyatt (New York: Oxford University Press, 1940), 111.

13. *Constitution on the Sacred Liturgy,* article 36.

14. *Una Sancta* 21:2 (St. Bartholomew, 1964), 4–6. See Henry Horn, "The English Language and Liturgical Modesty," *Response* 8:2 (St. Michael and All Angels, 1966), 106–10.

15. *Prayer Book Studies XVII: The Liturgy of the Lord's Supper* (New York: Church Hymnal Corporation, 1966), 54. See also Aidan Kavanagh, "Liturgy and Unity in the Light of Vatican II," *Una Sancta* 23:1 (Resurrection, 1966),

39; Kavanagh, "Cultural Diversity and Liturgical Language," *Una Sancta* 24:1 (Resurrection, 1967), 69–71.

16. See, however, Mary Rose D'Angelo, "*Abba* and 'Father': Imperial Theology and the Jesus Traditions," *Journal of Biblical Literature* 111:4 (Winter 1992), 614–22. Almost nothing seems agreed in biblical scholarship these days.

17. See Marianka Fousek, "Liturgy and Language," *Response* 7:1 (Pentecost, 1966), 29–30.

18. Donald Hall and Sven Birkerts, *Writing Well*, 8th ed. (New York: HarperCollins, 1994), 91, 108. Hall's language is "a change in style, however slight...."

19. See Brian Wren, *What Language Shall I Borrow? God-Talk in Worship: A Male Response to Feminist Theology* (New York: Crossroad, 1990).

20. Martin Luther, *Small Catechism*, the explanation of the Eighth Commandment: "We should fear and love God, and so we should not tell lies about our neighbor, nor betray, slander, or defame him, but should apologize for him, speak well of him, and interpret charitably all that he does."

21. The story is told that St. Lawrence the deacon of Rome (martyred 258), when he was commanded by the Roman prefect to hand over the church's treasure, assembled the poor and the sick and presented them to the prefect saying, "Here is the treasure of the church."

22. Neil Postman, *Amusing Ourselves to Death: Public Discourse in the Age of Show Business* (New York: Viking Penguin, 1986).

23. Martin Luther, "An Order of Mass and Communion for the Church at Wittenberg" (1523), *Luther's Works* (Philadelphia: Fortress Press, 1965), 53:19.

24. For example, a medieval woman, Birgitta (Bridget) of Sweden, whose feast day on the Roman and Lutheran calendars is July 23, was founder of the Order of the Holy Savior, an order of both men and women governed by an abbess (Whitby was an example in England of such a "double house" of monks and nuns ruled by a woman); boldly and repeatedly she told the popes to leave Avignon, where they had retreated, and to return to Rome, the city of which they were bishops. Catherine of Siena was another woman who told the pope where he ought to go.

Chapter Two – The Energy of Language

1. Martin Luther, *Small Catechism*, the explanation of the third article of the Apostles' Creed.

2. Quoted by Dominic Hibbard, "Extravagant and Exhausted Words," *Times Literary Supplement*, July 28–August 3, 1989.

3. Marghanita Laski, "Words — V," *Times Literary Supplement*, August 1, 1968, 882.

4. Gertrude Stein, *The Geographical History of America* (New York: Vintage Books, 1973 [1936]), 151.

5. Samuel Taylor Coleridge, "The Courier," August 10, 1811, *Essays on His Times in the Morning Post and the Courier,* vol. 2, ed. David V. Erdman (Princeton: Princeton University Press, 1978), 249. Coleridge also said, "For if words are not THINGS, they are LIVING POWERS, by which the things of most importance to mankind are actuated, combined, and harmonized" (*Aids to Reflection,* xvii).

6. Northrop Frye, *The Great Code: The Bible and Literature* (New York: Harcourt Brace Jovanovich, 1982), 11.

7. See ibid., 18.

8. It has been explained as the transfer of birth-giving from the womb of the female to a male equivalent, the mouth. See Joseph Campbell, *The Masks of God: Occidental Mythology* (New York: Viking Press, 1970), 157.

9. Charles Doria and Harris Lenowitz, eds. and trans., *Origins: Creation Texts from the Ancient Mediterranean* (Garden City, N.Y.: Anchor Books, 1976), 3–7; Campbell, *The Masks of God,* 83–85; John A. Wilson, "Egypt," in Henri Frankfort et al., eds., *Before Philosophy* (Baltimore: Penguin Books, 1949), 64–65; Mircea Eliade, *A History of Religious Ideas,* vol. 1: *From the Stone Age to the Eleusinian Mysteries,* trans. Willard R. Trask (Chicago: University of Chicago Press, 1978), 89–90.

10. Mircea Eliade, *From Primitives to Zen* (1967), no. 47, given in Eliade, *Gods, Goddesses, and Myths of Creation* (New York: Harper & Row, 1974), 86–87. See also Mircea Eliade, *Myth and Reality* trans. Willard R. Trask (New York: Harper & Row, 1968), 30; Eliade, *Patterns in Comparative Religion,* trans. Rosemary Sheed (Cleveland and New York: World Publishing Co., 1963), 410.

11. Eliade, *Myth and Reality,* 30–31.

12. See also the Anchor Bible translation by Jacob M. Myers ("even then I gave thought [to it]; these things were made by me and not by another"); the NRSV has less definitely, "then I planned these things, and they were made through me alone." See also the Winnebago story in Eliade, *Gods, Goddesses, and Myths of Creation,* no. 44, 83–84.

13. Frye, *The Great Code,* 6–7.

14. Eliade, *Myth and Reality,* 30–31.

15. Jean Piaget, *The Child's Conception of the World* (New York: Harcourt, Brace and Company, 1929), 72.

16. Edmund Jacob, *Theology of the Old Testament,* trans. Arthur W. Heathcote and Philip J. Allcock (New York: Harper & Brothers, 1958), 127.

17. Ethelbert Stauffer, *New Testament Theology,* trans. John Marsh (New York: Macmillan, 1956), 56.

18. Jacob, *Theology of the Old Testament,* 128.

19. William Barclay, *More New Testament Words* (New York: Harper & Bros., 1958), 113.

20. Ibid., 114.

21. Oscar Cullmann, *The Christology of the New Testament,* trans. Shirley C. Guthrie and Charles A. M. Hall (Philadelphia: Westminster Press, 1959), 255.

22. Michael Fishbane, *Text and Texture: Close Readings of Selected Biblical Texts* (New York: Schocken, 1979), 8.

23. Quoted in Jacob, *New Testament Theology*, 128.

24. Cullmann, *The Christology of the New Testament*, 259.

25. Barclay, *More New Testament Words*, 116.

26. It was not, however, universally so. In *Gilgamesh* Enkidu "called back the curse" he had put on the prostitute who had taught him civilization (*The Epic of Gilgamesh*, trans. N. K. Sandars [Baltimore: Penguin, 1964], 88).

27. See the insightful discussion of the passage in E. A. Speiser, *Genesis*, Anchor Bible 1 (Garden City, N.Y.: Doubleday and Co., 1964), 205–13.

28. See the *Talmud*, Baba Mezia 58b: verbal wrong is more heinous than monetary wrong because restoration is not possible for verbal wrong.

29. N. Scott Momaday, *The Way to Rainy Mountain* (New York: Ballantine Books, 1970), 42.

30. Ibid., 43.

31. See Robert Graves's poem "The Cool Web."

32. Louise Levertov, "A Note on the Work of the Imagination," *New Directions in Prose and Poetry #17* (New York: New Directions, 1961), 50.

33. See the discussion of the issues by Sara Maitland, "Children of the Book Come of Age," *Review of Books and Religion* (Fall 1990): 3ff; see also the letter by Ayla N. Bachman in the *New York Times*, March 7, 1989, which suggests that fiction is a Western form unknown in Islamic literature and that the Rushdie conflagration is the conflict between two worldviews alien to each other.

34. John Milton, "Areopagitica," *The Prose of John Milton*, ed. J. Max Patrick (Garden City, N.Y.: Doubleday, 1967), 271–72.

35. Jacques Maritain, "Language and the Theory of Sign," in Ruth Nanda Anshen, ed., *Language: An Enquiry into Its Meaning and Function* (New York: Harper and Row, 1957), 86, 89.

36. Donald Hall and Sven Birkerts, *Writing Well*, 8th ed. (New York: HarperCollins, 1994), 26.

37. R. P. Blackmur, *Language as Gesture* (New York: Harcourt, Brace and Co., 1952), chapter 1. His essay is in part a response to Kenneth Burke's examination of the language of poetry as symbolic action. See Kenneth Burke, *The Philosophy of Literary Form: Studies in Symbolic Action*, 3d ed. (Berkeley: University of California Press, 1974). Also to be noted is the interest at mid-century in gestural painting.

38. John Searle, *Speech-Acts: An Essay on the Philosophy of Language* (Cambridge: Cambridge University Press, 1969).

39. See *Liturgy* 5:1 (Summer 1985): 10.

40. John Austin, *How to Do Things with Words* (Cambridge, Mass.: Harvard University Press, 1962).

41. The ritual movements are described in Adrian Fortescue and J. B. O'Connell, *The Ceremonies of the Roman Rite Described*, 10th rev. ed. (London: Burns Oates & Washbourne, 1958 [1917]). For Anglican use, a standard

text was *Ritual Notes: A Comprehensive Guide to the Rites and Ceremonies of the Book of Common Prayer,* comp. Henry Cairncross and Edward C. R. Lamburn, 11th ed. (London: W. Knott, 1964).

42. See *A Cultural History of Gesture,* ed. Jan Bremmer and Herman Roodenburg (Ithaca: Cornell University Press, 1992).

43. On the history of this prayer see H. Boone Porter, "Be Present, Be Present," *Studia Liturgica* 21:2 (1991), 155–64.

44. *Lutheran Book of Worship,* Ministers Edition (Minneapolis and Philadelphia: Augsburg Publishing House and Board of Publication, Lutheran Church in America, 1978), 29, no. 34. The preparatory booklet was *Contemporary Worship 2: The Holy Communion* (Minneapolis: Augsburg Publishing House; Philadelphia: Board of Publication, Lutheran Church in America; St. Louis: Concordia Publishing House; 1970), 19, 36, 49, 64, 75.

45. Romano Guardini, letter to Johannes Wagner, *Herder Correspondence* August 1964, 237–39.

46. Augustine, *Confessions* 1:8. Ludwig Wittgenstein opens his *Philosophical Investigations* with this observation by Augustine.

47. Walter J. Ong, *The Presence of the Word* (New Haven: Yale University Press, 1967).

48. William A. Graham, *Beyond the Written Word: Oral Aspects of Scripture in the History of Religion* (Cambridge: Cambridge University Press, 1987), 9–10.

49. The work of the American composer John Cage (1912–92), particularly his silent piece 4'32", offers, to Western ears at least, an extreme example of the role of silence in music. See also his collection of essays, *Silence: Lectures and Writings* (Hanover, N.H.: University Press of New England, 1961).

50. Josef Pieper, *Leisure: the Basis of Culture* (New York: New American Library, 1963), 41.

51. Ibid..

52. Eric Fromm, *The Forgotten Language* (New York: Grove Press, 1957), 244–45.

53. Fishbane, *Text and Texture,* 9.

54. Carl Sandburg, *Good Morning, America* (New York: Harcourt, Brace and Co., 1928), vii.

55. T. S. Eliot, "Gerontion," line 18; also *Ash Wednesday* V (lines 152–53). See William Harmon, "T. S. Eliot's Raids on the Inarticulate," *PMLA* 91:3 (May 1976): 450–59.

56. Margot Astrov, *American Indian Prose and Poetry* (New York: Capricorn, 1962), 39 (originally published as *The Winged Serpent,* 1946). See Ohiyesa (Charles Alexander Eastman) in T. C. McLuhan ed., *Touch the Earth: A Self-Portrait of Indian Existence* (New York: Pocket Books, 1972), 110.

57. Susan Feldman, ed., *African Myths and Tales* (New York: Dell, 1970), 12.

58. R. P. Blackmur, "The Language of Silence," in Ruth Nanda Anshen, ed., *Language: An Enquiry into Its Meaning and Function* (New York: Harper & Bros., 1957), 152.

59. See Suzanne Guthrie, "Grace's Eyelet Veil," *Christian Century* 109:36 (December 2, 1992): 1099.

60. Ian Bradley, *Marching to the Promised Land: Has the Church a Future?* (London: John Murray, 1992): 219.

61. See Gustaf Aulen, *The Faith of the Christian Church*, trans. Eric H. Wahlstrom and G. Everett Arden (Philadelphia: Muhlenberg Press, 1948), 96–105.

62. Augustine, *Enarrationes in Psalmos*, Psalm 147, chapter 9 (commenting on verse 5, "Great is our Lord, and abundant in power; his understanding is beyond measure"): "conticescant humanae voces, requiescant humanae cogitationes; ad incomprehensibilia non se extendant quasi comprehensuri, sed tamquam participaturi." See *Nicene and Post-Nicene Fathers*, First Series, vol. 8 (Grand Rapids: Eerdmans, 1956), 667.

63. T. S. Eliot, *Burnt Norton* V, lines 149–53.

64. Samuel Johnson, "The Life of Waller," in *Lives of the English Poets*, 3 vols., ed. George Birkbeck Hill (New York: Octagon, 1967 [1905]), I, 291 #1136.

65. T. S. Eliot spoke of this office in connection with the work of a poet: "If, as we are aware, only part of the meaning can be conveyed by paraphrase, that is because the poet is occupied with the frontiers of consciousness beyond which words fail, though meanings still exist" ("The Music of Poetry," *On Poetry and Poets* [New York: Farrar, Straus and Cudahy, 1957], 22–23).

Chapter Three – Poetry: Allusive Language

1. G. K. Chesterton, *Orthodoxy* (New York: John Lane, 1908), 48.

2. C. Day Lewis, *The Lyric Impulse* (Cambridge: Harvard University Press, 1965), 24.

3. Ibid., 12.

4. Ibid., 5.

5. Ibid., 24.

6. See Barbara Hardy, *The Advantage of Lyric* (Bloomington: Indiana University Press, 1977). See also Andrew Welsh, *Roots of Lyric* (Princeton: Princeton University Press, 1978); W. R. Johnson, *The Idea of Lyric: Lyric Modes in Ancient and Modern Poetry* (Berkeley: University of California Press, 1982).

7. Day Lewis, *The Lyric Impulse*, 26.

8. This is the text of stanza three as given in the *Hymnal 1940* (no. 20) and stanza four in the *Common Service Book* (no. 20) and the *Service Book and Hymnal* (no. 17). In the *Lutheran Book of Worship* (no. 42) and the *Hymnal 1982* (no. 82) the opening words have been weakened to "Let the heights of heaven adore him," doubtless to avoid the archaic "O ye" but thereby losing the direct address to the heights of heaven (presumably the angel host.)

9. Translation by John Ellerton as given in the *Oxford American Hymnal*

for Schools and Colleges, ed. Carl F. Pfatteicher (New York: Oxford University Press, 1930), no. 367, and *Service Book and Hymnal* (no. 93). The hymn is altered in the *Hymnal 1982* and botched in the *Lutheran Book of Worship.*

10. The translation is by John Mason Neale, "A Great and Mighty Wonder," given in the *Service Book and Hymnal* (no. 18).

11. The *Hymnal 1982,* no. 165, 166 stanza 3.

12. The hymn begins, "This is my Father's world."

13. Day Lewis, *The Lyric Impulse,* 4.

14. See the impressive description of this process by William James and by Alfred North Whitehead given in Walker Gibson, ed., *The Limits of Language* (New York: Hill and Wang, 1962), 8–14.

15. Robert Scholes, *Elements of Poetry* (New York: Oxford University Press, 1969), 3.

16. Elizabeth Drew, *Poetry: A Modern Guide to Its Understanding and Enjoyment* (New York: Dell, 1959), 31–32.

17. John Keats, Letter to John Taylor, February 27, 1818.

18. Robert Frost, "The Figure a Poem Makes," an introductory essay Frost wrote for an enlarged edition of his *Collected Poems* (1939) and afterward consistently included in comprehensive collections of his poetry, given in Elaine Barry, *Robert Frost on Writing* (New Brunswick, N.J.: Rutgers University Press, 1973), 126.

19. Ernst Cassirer, *An Essay on Man* (New York: Bantam Books, 1970 [1944]), 158.

20. Ibid., 250.

21. C. M. Bowra, *Primitive Song* (Cleveland: World Publishing Co., 1962), 145.

22. Ibid., 14.

23. Ibid., 279.

24. T. S. Eliot, "The Music of Poetry," *On Poetry and Poets* (New York: Farrar, Straus and Cudahy, 1957), 32.

25. Bowra, *Primitive Song,* 30.

26. Ibid., 286.

27. See Margot Astrov, *American Indian Prose and Poetry* (New York: Capricorn, 1962), 21; George W. Cronyn, *American Indian Poetry* (New York: Liveright, 1962 [1934]), xvi, 139; James Anderson Winn, *Unsuspected Eloquence: A History of the Relations between Poetry and Music* (New Haven: Yale University Press, 1984), 2–14; Andrew Welsh, *Roots of Lyric: Primitive Poetry and Modern Poetics* (Princeton: Princeton University Press, 1978).

28. Bowra, *Primitive Song,* 28, 264–65.

29. Ibid., 29.

30. Robert Scholes and Carl H. Klaus, *Elements of Drama* (New York: Oxford University Press, 1971), 17.

31.   Spring up, O well! — Sing to it! —
                     the well that the leaders sank,

that the nobles of the people dug,
with the scepter, with the staff.
32. Astrov, *American Indian Prose and Poetry*, 15.

33. See Peter Pouncey, "On a Background for Teachers," in Chester E. Finn, Jr., Diane Ravitch, and Robert T. Fancher, eds., *Against Mediocrity: The Humanities in America's High Schools* (New York: Holmes and Meier, 1984), 135–37.

34. George W. Cronyn, ed., *American Indian Poetry: An Anthology of Songs and Chants* (New York: Liveright, 1962), 360.

35. Donald Hall, *Writing Well*, 3d ed. (Boston: Little Brown, 1979), 264.

36. Astrov, *American Indian Prose and Poetry*, 19.

37. Richmond Lattimore, trans., *Greek Lyrics*, 2d ed. (Chicago: University of Chicago Press, 1960), 56.

38. John Moore, ed., *Greek Lyric Poets* (Cambridge, Mass.: Harvard University Press, 1947), 104.

39. Lattimore, *Greek Lyrics*, 149.

40. Augustine of Hippo, *Discourse on Psalm 148*, 1–2, trans. in the *Liturgy of the Hours*, 2:864–65, the Second Reading in the Office of Readings for Saturday of the Fifth Week of Easter. See also James McKinnon, ed., *Music in Early Christian Literature* (New York: Cambridge University Press, 1987), nos. 362, 363.

41. James Anderson Winn, *Unsuspected Eloquence: A History of the Relations between Poetry and Music* (New Haven: Yale University Press, 1981), 35.

42. See Jane Parry Tompkins, ed., *Reader-Response Criticism* (Baltimore: Johns Hopkins University Press, 1981). For a helpful review of modern literary theory see Terry Eagleton, *Literary Theory: An Introduction* Minneapolis: University of Minnesota Press, 1983).

43. Wolfgang Iser, *The Implied Reader* (Baltimore: Johns Hopkins University Press, 1974), 274–75.

44. Ibid., 275. Iser is aware that the process has been understood for some time. He quotes (275) the eighteenth-century novelist Laurence Sterne, who says in *Tristam Shandy* (London, 1956, II, 11.79), "The truest respect which you can pay to the reader's understanding is to halve the matter amicably, and leave him something to imagine, in his turn, as well as yourself. For my part, I am eternally paying him compliments of this kind, and do all that lies in my power to keep his imagination as busy as my own."

45. Ibid., 279. Reader-response criticism is not all of one piece. Iser and Louise Rosenblatt emphasize the interaction between the text and the reader; David Bleich the way the reader projects his or her own desires on a text; Stanley Fish the communal assumptions that control the sorts of attention we pay to texts and thereby shape our readings of them.

46. See *Christianity and Literature* 36:4 (Summer 1987): 13–32; C. David Benson, "Chaucer's Unfinished Pilgrimage," *Christianity and Literature* 37:4 (Summer 1988): 7–22, especially 15.

47. See Robert Scholes, *Protocols of Reading* (New Haven: Yale University Press, 1989).

48. E. B. White, "Calculating Machine," *Poems and Sketches* (New York: Harper and Row, 1951), 239.

49. Stephen Prickett, *Words and "The Word": Language, Poetics and Biblical Interpretation* (Cambridge: Cambridge University Press, 1986), 7.

50. Ibid., 10.

51. Ibid., 13.

52. C. H. Sisson, "Turning Points in Consciousness," *Times Literary Supplement*, January 30, 1987, 116.

53. Prickett, *Words and "The Word,"* 7.

54. Ibid., 7–8.

55. Ibid., 9. The quotation is from Ward Allen, ed., *Translating for King James* (New York: Penguin, 1970), 89. Bois's reference is to the word "praise" in 1 Peter 1:7, which might refer either to Jesus or to the church members.

56. Prickett, *Words and "The Word,"* 8.

57. Ibid., 9.

58. Ernst Cassirer, *An Essay on Man* (New York: Bantam Books, 1970 [1944]), 13.

59. Northrop Frye, *The Great Code* (New York: Harcourt Brace Jovanovich, 1982), 218.

60. Alfred North Whitehead, *The Concept of Nature* (Cambridge: Cambridge University Press, 1920), 163.

61. Chesterton, *Orthodoxy*, 48–49.

62. Richard H. Fogle, "A Note on the Ode to a Nightingale," *Modern Language Quarterly* 8 (1947): 81.

63. Mircea Eliade, *Images and Symbols: Studies in Religious Symbolism*, trans. Philip Mairet (New York: Sheed and Ward, 1969), 11.

64. Ibid., 12.

65. Mircea Eliade, *A History of Religious Ideas*, vol. 1: *From the Stone Age to the Eleusinian Mysteries*, trans. Willard R. Trask (Chicago: University of Chicago Press, 1978), 270. See also C. M. Bowra, *The Greek Experience* (New York: New American Library, 1957), 133.

66. Eliade, *History of Religious Ideas*, 1:279–80.

67. Peter Chrysologos, *Sermon 160*, translated in *The Liturgy of the Hours* (New York: Catholic Book Publishing Co., 1975), 1:577–78.

68. See the chapter on symbol in Umberto Eco, *Semiotics and the Philosophy of Language* (New York: Macmillan, 1984), 143–46.

69. For an account of the allegorical interpretation of the mass, see Josef A. Jungmann, *The Mass of the Roman Rite: Its Origins and Development*, trans. Francis A. Brunner, revised by Charles K. Riepe (New York: Benziger Bros., 1961), 8, 67, 81–85, 88.

70. Derek Travers, "Langland's *Piers Plowman*," in Boris Ford, ed., *Medieval Literature: Chaucer and the Alliterative Tradition* (New York: Penguin, 1982), 191.

71. M. H. Abrams et al., eds., *Norton Anthology of English Literature*, 6th ed. (New York: W. W. Norton Co., 1993), 1:364.

72. As, for example, it frustrated the great medievalist Albert C. Baugh in the work of which he is the editor, *A Literary History of England* (New York: Appleton-Century-Crofts, 1948), 244: "Read for the individual visions and scenes the poem is genuinely absorbing, but it is the despair of anyone who seeks in it a completely orderly plan or logical development from episode to episode."

73. Beryl Smalley, *The Study of the Bible in the Middle Ages* (New York: Oxford University Press, 1941), 218. Jean Petit, a Parisian master of theology, in a speech justifying the murder in 1407 of the Duke of Orleans, the king's brother, asserted, "c'est-à-dire que tenir le sens litéral en la Sainte Ecriture est occîre son âme" ("Always to keep the literal sense of Holy Scripture means to kill its soul"). Quoted in Earl Miner, ed., *The Literary Uses of Typology from the Late Middle Ages to the Present* (Princeton: Princeton University Press, 1977), 29.

74. Robert T. Grant, *A Short History of the Interpretation of the Bible*, rev. ed. (New York: Macmillan, 1963), 121.

75. Eco, *Semiotics and the Philosophy of Language*, 147–53.

76. Karlfried Froelich in Miner, *The Literary Uses of Typology*, 20ff.

77. John Cassian, *Conferences* (*Collationes*) 14:8.

78. See Thomas Aquinas, *Summa Theologica*, part I, question 1, question 10; Dante, *Letter to Can Grande*, paragraphs 7, 8.

79. See Barbara Leah Harman, "Conclusion: The Bible as Counter-Text," *Costly Monuments: Representations of the Self in George Herbert's Poetry* (Cambridge: Harvard University Press, 1982).

80. See Charles E. Hambrick-Stowe, *The Practice of Piety: Puritan Devotional Disciplines in Seventeenth-century New England* (Chapel Hill: University of North Carolina Press, 1982), chaps. 3 and 7.

81. Wallace Stevens, "Adagia," *Opus Posthumous* [sic], ed. Samuel French Morse (New York: Knopf, 1957), 175.

82. Wallace Stevens, "Sunday Morning," lines 17–18.

83. Jon Whitman, *Allegory: The Dynamics of an Ancient and Medieval Technique* (Cambridge: Harvard University Press, 1987), 1.

84. Ibid., 13.

85. V. A. Kolve, *Chaucer and the Imagery of Narrative: The First Five Canterbury Tales* (Palo Alto, Calif.: Stanford University Press, 1984), 10.

86. This schema takes its point of departure from Alhazen's anatomy of the human eye. Noted by A. J. Minnis in "Light in the Interior Eye," *Times Literary Supplement*, August 3, 1984, 865.

87. *The Prose of John Milton*, ed. J. Max Patrick (Garden City, N.Y.: Doubleday, 1967), 318.

Chapter Four – Music: Transcendent Language

1. See Carol Doran and Thomas H. Troeger, "Recognizing an Ancient Unity: Music and Liturgy as Complemental Disciplines," *Worship* 60:5 (September 1966): 386–98. For the importance of music in a larger context, see Joyce Irwin, ed., *Sacred Sound: Music in Religious Thought and Practice* (Decatur, Ga.: Scholars Press, 1986).

2. "Song," *Oxford Companion to Music* (New York: Oxford University Press, 1970), 966.

3. Philip Wheelwright, *The Burning Fountain* (Bloomington: Indiana University Press, 1954), 3.

4. Ibid., 16.

5. Ralph P. Martin, *Worship in the Early Church*, rev. ed. (Grand Rapids: Eerdmans, 1975 [1964]), 39.

6. Athanasius, *The Life of Antony and the Letter to Marcellinus*, trans. Robert C. Gregory (New York: Paulist Press, 1980), 23.

7. Natalie Curtis, *The Indians' Book: Songs and Legends of the American Indians* (New York: Dover, 1968 [1907]), 39.

8. Margot Astrov, *American Indian Prose and Poetry* (New York: Capricorn, 1962), 202 (first published as *The Winged Serpent*, 1946).

9. Gloria Levitas, Frank Robert Vivelo, and Jacqueline J. Vivelo, eds., *American Indian Prose and Poetry: We Wait in the Darkness* (New York: Capricorn, 1974), 107.

10. Astrov, *American Indian Prose and Poetry*, 175.

11. George W. Cronyn ed., *American Indian Poetry* (New York: Liveright, 1962 [1918]), 19.

12. Ruth Underhill, *Singing for Power: The Song Magic of the Papago Indians of Southern Arizona* (Berkeley: University of California Press, 1938), 5.

13. Nathan Mitchell, "Amen Corner: The Life of the Dead," *Worship* 66:6 (1992), 537.

14. See, for example, Aristotle, *De Caelo* 2.9.

15. Clement of Alexandria, *Paedagogus* 2.4, given as no. 54 in James McKinnon, *Music in Early Christian Literature* (New York: Cambridge University Press, 1987), 33–34.

16. Clement of Alexandria, *Stromata* 7.16.102, given in McKinnon, no. 62.

17. Clement of Alexandria, *Protrepticus* 1.5.3–7.3, given in McKinnon, no. 45. See also Oliver Strunk, *Source Readings in Music History from Classical Antiquity through the Romantic Era* (New York: Norton, 1950), 59–63.

18. Clement of Alexandria, *Paedagogus* 2.4, given in McKinnon, no. 52.

19. John Chrysostom, *In psalmum xli, 2*, given in McKinnon, no. 169.

20. Jerome, *Commentarium in epistulam ad Ephesios* 3.5.19, given in McKinnon, no. 333.

21. Johan Huizinga, *Homo Ludens: A Study of the Play Element in Culture* (Boston: Beacon Press, 1955), 127.

22. Ibid., 127.

23. Joseph Gelineau, *Voices and Instruments in Christian Worship*, trans. Clifford Howell (Collegeville, Minn.: Liturgical Press, 1964), 44.

24. C. M. Bowra, *Primitive Song* (Cleveland and New York: World Publishing Co., 1962), 36.

25. Mark W. Booth, *The Experience of Song* (New Haven: Yale University Press, 1981), 201.

26. Victor Zuckerkandl, *Sound and Symbol: Music and the External World*, trans. Willard R. Trask (New York: Pantheon Books, 1956), 1.

27. "Lyric Poetry, Greek," in D. R. Dudley and D. M. Lang, eds., *Penguin Companion to Literature* 4 (Baltimore: Penguin Books, 1969), 110.

28. Yüan Mei in Cyril Birch, ed., *Anthology of Chinese Literature* (New York: Grove Press, 1972), 2:193.

29. Bowra, *Primitive Song*, 276.

30. Ibid., 276.

31. Jonathan Edwards, *Personal Narrative*, given in Philip H. Pfatteicher, *Festivals and Commemorations* (Minneapolis: Augsburg Publishing House, 1980), 130–31.

32. Quoted in Sylvan Barnet, Morton Berman, and William Burto, eds., *An Introduction to Literature*, expanded edition (New York: HarperCollins, 1994), 730.

33. See the discussion in Booth, *The Experience of Song*, 198–99.

34. Ibid., 201.

35. Bowra, *The Primitive Song*, 28.

36. Booth, *The Experience of Song*, 7.

37. Ibid., 7.

38. Ibid., 8.

39. Victor Zuckerkandl, *Sound and Symbol: Music and the External World*, trans. Willard R. Trask (New York: Pantheon Books, 1956), 71.

40. Ibid., 51.

41. Ibid., 42.

42. Booth, *The Experience of Song*, 18.

43. Ibid., 18.

44. Ibid., 20; the quotation is from Zuckerkandl.

45. Zuckerkandl, *Sound and Symbol*, 70.

46. Booth, *The Experience of Song*, 14.

47. Ibid., 15.

48. Ibid.

49. Elie Wiesel, *The Gates of the Forest*, trans. Frances Frenaye (New York: Schocken, 1982), 200–203.

50. Marshall Brown, "Unheard Melodies: The Force of Form," *PMLA* 107 (1992): 466. The concluding thoughts in this chapter have been suggested in large measure by Brown's stimulating essay.

51. James Joyce, "The Dead," *Dubliners* (New York: Penguin, 1991), 221.

52. Brown, "Unheard Melodies," 474.

53. Ibid., 475.
54. Ibid., 477.
55. Ibid., 479.

Chapter Five – The Necessity of Continuity

1. Eivind Berggrav, *Land of Suspense* (Minneapolis: Augsburg Publishing House, 1943), 84. Jane McLoughlin, "Saving the Sacred Wood," *Manchester Guardian Weekly*, September 17, 1989, tells a different story of the perspective enforced by trees: "My father, who lived off the land, used to send me as a combative brat to dispel all kinds of childish anger by kicking a tree. It worked. Counting to 10 or banging a pillow or beating up a sister did not work. The tree invariably imposed a sense of perspective, a metaphysical symbol of the absurdity of human aggression."

2. Kim Taplin, *Tongues in Trees* (Hartland, Bideford, Devon: Green Books, 1989), 19.

3. Isaiah 55:10–11; Matthew 13:3–23; Mark 4:3–20; Luke 8:5–15.

4. Matthew 13:31–32; Mark 4:30–32; Luke 13:18–19.

5. The interrelationship between humanity and trees is deep and profound. "The devastation of the English tree population in the 1987 gales and the ravages of Dutch elm disease share the sense of cosmic emotional desecration of the bombing of Dresden and the threatened extinction of the African elephant. For centuries conquerors have underlined their conquest of the vanquished by tearing down their trees. This is a practical (it saves a valuable domestic product) and a symbolic gesture, the ruthless deprivation of national pride demonstrated by the Japanese in once-forested Korea and long ago by the English in Ireland" (McLoughlin,"Saving the Sacred Wood")..

6. T. S. Eliot, *After Strange Gods: A Primer of Modern Heresy* (New York: Harcourt, Brace and Co., 1934), 32, 25.

7. Eusebius, *History of the Church* 5.23.24.

8. Mircea Eliade, *Cosmos and History: The Myth of the Eternal Return*, trans. Willard R. Trask (New York: Harper and Row, 1959), 86.

9. Algernon Charles Swinburne, "When the Hounds of Spring," from *Atalanta in Calydon*, line 2.

10. Eliade, *Cosmos and History*, 86.

11. Joseph Campbell, *The Masks of God*, vol. 2: *Oriental Mythology* (New York: Viking, 1962), 255.

12. Joseph Campbell, *The Masks of God*, vol. 3: *Occidental Mythology* (New York: Viking, 1964), 9.

13. Mircea Eliade, *Patterns in Comparative Religion* (Cleveland and New York: World Publishing Co., 1963), 154.

14. Eliade, *Cosmos and History*, 86–90, 141–47. The book was first pub-

lished in English (reflecting the French title) as *The Myth of the Eternal Return* (1954).

15. Philip Wheelwright, *The Burning Fountain: A Study in the Language of Symbolism* (Bloomington: Indiana University Press, 1954), 8.

16. Philip Wheelwright, "Poetry, Myth, and Reality," in Allen Tate, ed., *The Language of Poetry* (New York: Russell and Russell, 1960), 10, describes "the very essence of myth" as "that haunting awareness of transcendental forces peering through the cracks of the visible universe."

17. Eliade, *Patterns*, 155.

18. Ibid., 158.

19. Ibid., 160.

20. Campbell, *Oriental Mythology*, 91.

21. Eliade, *Patterns*, 162.

22. Ibid.

23. Ibid., 163.

24. Ibid., 164.

25. Ibid.

26. Ibid.

27. Ibid.

28. Ibid., 171.

29. Ibid., 172.

30. Ibid., 176.

31. Ibid., 181.

32. Ibid., 157.

33. Ibid., 156.

34. Campbell, *Oriental Mythology*, 91.

35. Campbell, *Occidental Mythology*, 9.

36. Ibid., 10.

37. Eliade, *Patterns*, 184.

38. Ibid.

39. Robert McAfee Brown, "Abraham Heschel: A Passion for Sincerity," *Christianity and Crisis* 33:21 (December 10, 1973): 259.

40. Anselm, *Proslogion* I: "Neque enim quaero intelligere ut credam, sed credo ut intelligam." Given in M. J. Charlesworth, trans., *St. Anselm's Proslogion* (Oxford: Clarendon Press, 1965), 114–15.

41. Paul Ricoeur, *The Symbolism of Evil* (Boston: Beacon Press, 1969), 351.

42. Thomas Henry Huxley, "Agnosticism and Christianity," *Essays on Some Controverted Questions* (1892). Arthur Hugh Clough was more circumspect in his skepticism; in a letter to his sister in 1847 he wrote of the Atonement, "I think others are more right who say boldly, we don't understand it, and therefore we won't fall down and worship it. Though there is no occasion for adding — 'there *is* nothing in it' — I should say, until I know, I will wait, and if I am not born with the power to discover, I will do what I can . . . and neither pretend to know, nor, without knowing, pretend to embrace: nor yet oppose those who, by whatever means, are increasing or trying to increase knowledge."

Given in M. H. Abrams et al., eds., *Norton Anthology of English Literature*, 6th ed. (New York: W. W. Norton, 1993), 2:1451.

43. Percy Bysshe Shelley, *A Defense of Poetry* (1821).

44. John S. Dunne, *A Search for God in Time and Memory* (New York: Macmillan, 1969), 7.

45. G. K. Chesterton, *Orthodoxy* (London: John Lane, 1908), 151.

46. E. A. Speiser, *Genesis*, Anchor Bible 1 (Garden City, N.Y.: Doubleday, 1964), 45.

47. Ibid., 46.

48. Chesterton, *Orthodoxy*, 148–49, 150.

49. *Lutheran Book of Worship*, the Prayer of the Day for the Fourth Sunday after the Epiphany.

Chapter Six – Worship and Christian Formation

1. Collect for the Twenty-Sixth Sunday after Trinity in the *Church Book* (1868), the *Common Service Book* (1917), the *Service Book and Hymnal* (1958), translated from the *Evangeliebok* (1639) of the Church of Sweden, revised in the *Lutheran Book of Worship* (1978): "Lord God, so rule and govern our hearts and minds by your Holy Spirit that, always keeping in mind the end of all things and the day of judgment, we may be stirred up to holiness of life here and may live with you forever in the world to come, through your Son, Jesus Christ our Lord."

2. Preface for Advent in the *Service Book and Hymnal* and the *Lutheran Book of Worship*.

3. Paraphrase by Howard Chandler Robbins (1876–1952) in *The Hymnal 1982* (no. 163).

4. General Thanksgiving, *Book of Common Prayer*, 59, 72, 101, 125; *Lutheran Book of Worship*, Ministers Edition, 112.

5. Augustine, Exposition of Psalm 32; sermon 1.7: "Let us sing a new song not with our lips but with our lives."

6. Nelson Goodman, *Languages of Art: An Approach to a Theory of Symbols* (Indianapolis and New York: Bobbs-Merrill Co., 1968), 259.

7. Robert N. Bellah et al., *Habits of the Heart: Individualism and Commitment in American Life* (New York: Harper & Row, 1985). See M. Francis Mannion, "Liturgy and the Present Crisis of Culture," *Worship* 62 (1988): 98–103.

8. See as an example David L. Miller, "What's Good and Bad about Lutheran Worship?" *The Lutheran* 1:5 (March 16, 1988): 10–12.

9. For a sharp presentation of such demands see Paul G. Johnson, "Making a Real Return to Church Possible," *Christian Century* 104:22 (July 29–August 5, 1987): 656–59.

10. Martin Luther, *Large Catechism*, The Sacrament of the Altar, 65, in *The*

Book of Concord, ed. Theodore G. Tappert et al. (Philadelphia: Muhlenberg Press, 1959), 454.

11. *The Book of Concord,* 352.

12. Johnson, "Making a Real Return to Church Possible," 657.

13. Joseph Sittler, *Gravity and Grace: Reflections and Provocations,* ed. Linda-Marie Delloff (Minneapolis: Augsburg Publishing House, 1986), 95, 97. Certain schools of modern literary criticism would take issue with Sittler's assertion, but an objection to Reader-Response criticism is that it may, if taken to extremes, destroy any objectivity a text possesses.

14. Wendy Doniger O'Flaherty, "The Aims of Education Address," delivered September 23, 1985, University of Chicago *Record* 20:1 (April 10, 1986): 44.

15. Harold Bloom, "Literature as the Bible," *New York Review of Books* March 31, 1988, 25.

16. Janet Lembke, *Dangerous Birds: A Naturalist's Aviary* (New York: Lyons and Burford, 1992).

17. Sue Hubbell, "Admonished by Grackles," *New York Times Book Review* October 11, 1992, 14.

18. See the *Book of Common Prayer,* 47–49, 88–90, and the *Lutheran Book of Worship,* Canticle 18, for three translations of the great song of creation.

19. *Lutheran Book of Worship,* Ministers Edition, 145.

20. Edward Foley, Kathleen Hughes, and Gilbert Ostdiek, "The Preparatory Rites: A Case Study in Liturgical Ecology," *Worship* 67:1 (1993): 31. See also John A. T. Robinson, *Liturgy Coming to Life* (Philadelphia: Westminster, 1964), 62, 90; Philip H. Pfatteicher and Carlos R. Messerli, *Manual on the Liturgy* (Minneapolis: Augsburg Publishing House, 1979), 232; Philip H. Pfatteicher, *Commentary on the Lutheran Book of Worship: Lutheran Liturgy in Its Ecumenical Context* (Minneapolis: Fortress, 1990), 155.

21. Foley et al., *The Preparatory Rites,* 22.

22. Ibid., 30.

23. Mark Searle, "The Uses of Liturgical Language," *Liturgy: Language and Metaphor (Liturgy* 4:4, Spring 1985): 15–19.

24. The translation of the Nicene Creed by the International Consultation on English Texts that shifted from "I believe" to the plural "We believe" has helped make clear that the creed is a statement of the faith of the church rather than a personal declaration.

25. Searle, "The Use of Liturgical Language," 18.

26. Martin Luther, "An Exposition of the Lord's Prayer," *Luther's Works* (Philadelphia: Fortress Press, 1969), 42:20.

27. John Chrysostom, *In psalmum xli,* 2. Given in McKinnon, no. 168

28. Dietrich Bonhoeffer, *Life Together,* trans. John W. Doberstein (New York: Harper, 1954), 84.

29. Searle, "The Use of Liturgical Language," 18.

30. Cyprian, *On the Lord's Prayer* 11. See *Ante-Nicene Fathers* (Grand Rapids: Eerdmans, 1957), 5:450.

31. "Neque enim quaero intelligere ut credam, sed credo ut intelligam." Anselm, *Proslogion* I, given in M. J. Charlesworth trans., *St. Anselm's* Proslogion (Oxford: Clarendon Press, 1965), 114–15.

32. Martin Luther, "Preface to the Psalter," *Luther's Works* (Philadelphia: Fortress Press, 1960), 35:255, 256–57.

33. *Lutheran Book of Worship*, 74, 94, 117.

34. John W. Doberstein, *Minister's Prayer Book*, rev. Philip H. Pfatteicher (Philadelphia: Fortress Press, 1986), 224, 259–60, 313, 339–40, 368–69, 393–94, 436.

35. Ibid., 186–87.

36. Goodman, *Languages of Art*, 259.

37. Ibid., 259–60.

38. Donald Hall and Sven Birkerts, *Writing Well*, 8th ed. (New York: HarperCollins, 1994), 4.

39. Ibid., 8.

40. Michael Frayn, *Constructions* (London: Wildwood House, 1974), no. 219.

41. Mannion, "Liturgy and the Present Crisis of Culture," 121–22.

42. *Lutheran Book of Worship*, Offertory, 66, 86, 107.

Chapter Seven – Beyond the Boundaries

1. Samuel Johnson, Preface to his *Dictionary of the English Language* (1755): change being irresistible, "it remains that we retard what we cannot repel.... Tongues, like governments, have a natural tendency to degeneration; we have long preserved our constitution, let us make some struggles for our language" (*Johnson's Dictionary: A Modern Selection*, ed. E. L. McAdam, Jr. and George Milne [New York: Pantheon, 1963], 27).

2. Two Lutheran church bodies addressed themselves to these concerns and issued booklets of guidelines: *English Language Guidelines for Using Inclusive Liturgical Language in the Lutheran Church in America* (Philadelphia: Division for Parish Services of the Lutheran Church in America, 1976) and *Guidelines for Avoiding Bias in Publications of the American Lutheran Church* (Minneapolis: Publication Development Division of Augsburg Publishing House, 1978). The Office of the Secretary and the Commission for Communication of the Evangelical Lutheran Church in America (a merger of the American Lutheran Church, the Association of Evangelical Lutheran Churches, and the Lutheran Church in America) produced *Guidelines for Inclusive Use of the English Language for Speakers, Writers, and Editors* (Chicago: ELCA Commission for Communication, 1989). The reaction to these publications, particularly the last, was decidedly mixed.

3. See, for example, Casey Miller and Kate Swift, *Words and Women* (New York: Doubleday, 1976); Francine Wattman Frank and Paula A. Treichler, *Lan-*

guage, Gender, and Professional Writing: Theoretical Approaches and Guidelines for Nonsexist Usage (New York: Modern Language Association, 1989).

4. In the *Lutheran Book of Worship* (hymn 551) and in the *Hymnal 1982* (no. 376) the troublesome stanza is omitted.

5. In the version in the *Lutheran Book of Worship* (hymn 210) the line has been improved by replacing "dark" with "dread"; moreover, "his sword" becomes "the sword" (angels are genderless), although to whom the sword belongs is made somewhat less clear. *The Hymnal 1982* leaves the line unchanged.

6. It is, however, not simply a matter of modernization. Women are excluded from the Maundy Thursday action of foot-washing in the present Roman rite, but it was not always so; the limitation to males is an aberration of the reformed rite of 1969. See Peter Jeffrey, "Mandatum Novum Do Vobis: Toward a Renewal of the Holy Thursday Footwashing Rite," *Worship* 64:2 (1990): 107–41, especially 134.

7. Donald Hall and Sven Birkerts, *Writing Well*, 8th ed. (New York: Harper-Collins, 1994), 83. See also Christopher B. Ricks, *T. S. Eliot and Prejudice* (Berkeley: University of California Press, 1988), 77ff.

8. See Robert W. Jenson, *The Triune Identity: God according to the Gospel* (Philadelphia: Fortress Press, 1982); Catherine Mowry LaCugna, *God for Us: The Trinity and Christian Life* (San Francisco: HarperSanFrancisco, 1992); Catherine Mowry LaCugna, "The Baptismal Formula, Feminist Objections, and Trinitarian Theology," *Journal of Ecumenical Studies* 26:2 (Spring 1989): 235–50; Geoffrey Wainwright, "The Doctrine of the Trinity: Where the Church Stands or Falls," *Interpretation* 45:2 (April 1991): 117–21; Barbara Brown Zikmund, "The Trinity and Women's Experience," *Christian Century* 104:12 (April 15, 1987): 354–56; Roland M. Frye, *Language for God and Feminist Language* (Princeton: Center for Theological Inquiry, 1988).

9. Tryggve N. D. Mettinger, *In Search of God: The Meaning and Message of the Everlasting Names*, trans. Frederick H. Cryer (Philadelphia: Fortress Press, 1988), 11.

10. Christopher R. Seitz, "Reader Competence and the Offense of Biblical Language: The Limitations of So-called Inclusive Language," *Pro Ecclesia* 2:2 (Spring 1993): 143–49.

11. Martin Luther, *The Large Catechism*, given in *The Book of Concord*, ed. Theodore G. Tappert et al. (Philadelphia: Muhlenberg Press, 1959), 368.

12. Brevard S. Childs, "Is the God of the Old Testament a Male Deity?" in *Old Testament Theology in a Canonical Context* (Philadelphia: Fortress Press, 1985), 39–40.

13. George Lindbeck, *The Nature of Doctrine* (Philadelphia: Westminster Press, 1984), 34.

14. See Susan D. Cohen, "Colette's *Gigi* and the Politics of Naming," *PMLA* 100:5 (October 1985): 805 n. 1.

15. Sallie McFague, *Metaphorical Theology: Models of God in Religious Language* (Philadelphia: Fortress Press, 1982), 13.

16. T. S. Eliot, *Little Gidding*, line 127.

17. Luther Reed, "A Pan-Lutheran Liturgy and Hymnal," *Response* 7:4 (1966): 207.

18. John Bunyan, *The Pilgrim's Progress* (New York: Penguin, 1987), 107.

19. Jacques Le Goff, *The Birth of Purgatory*, trans. Arthur Goldhammer (Chicago: University of Chicago Press, 1984), 359.

20. Stephen Prickett, *Words and the Word: Language, Poetics, and Biblical Interpretation* (Cambridge: Cambridge University Press, 1986), 32.

21. The appeal for the reappearance of a formative figure of the past is not limited to liturgists. Mina Shaughnessy, the student of rhetoric and composition, declared that in our present linguistic plight, "academic rhetoric . . . is waiting for an Aristotle" (Mina Shaughnessy, "Some Needed Research in Writing," *College Composition and Communication* 28 [December 1977]: 320).

22. R. S. Thomas, "A Frame for Poetry," *The Times Literary Supplement*, March 3, 1966, 169. See also James B. Twitchell, *Carnival Culture: The Trashing of Taste in America* (New York: Columbia University Press, 1992).

23. C. Day Lewis, *The Lyric Impulse* (Cambridge: Harvard University Press, 1965), 23.

24. Ibid., 24.

25. Peter R. Pouncey, "The Nerve to be a Writer," *Amherst* 42:1 (Fall 1989): 19.

26. See Margaret Doody's perceptive attack on modern liturgy, " 'How Shall We Sing the Lord's Song upon an Alien Soil?': The New Episcopalian Liturgy," in Leonard Michaels and Christopher Ricks, eds., *The State of the Language* (Berkeley: University of California Press, 1980), 108–24, and her devastating attack on modern rewriting of hymns, "Changing What We Sing," in Leonard Michaels and Christopher Ricks, eds., *The State of the Language* (Berkeley: University of California Press, 1990), 315–40.

27. George Steiner, *Language and Silence: Essays on Language and Literature and the Inhuman* (New York: Athenaeum, 1970), 31.

28. T. S. Eliot, *George Herbert: Writers and Their Work*, no. 152 (London: Longmans, Green, 1962), 25.

29. The conclusion of Archibald MacLeish, "Ars Poetica."

30. Frank Kermode, "John," in Robert Alter and Frank Kermode, eds., *Literary Guide to the Bible* (Cambridge, Mass.: Harvard University Press, 1987), 450.

31. Peter Galazda, "The Role of Icons in Byzantine Worship," *Studia Liturgica* 21:2 (1991): 127. The reference is to Eusebius, *Historia Ecclesiastica* 427.

32. Petro B. T. Bilaniuk quoted in Galazda, "The Role of Icons," 128.

33. Galazda, "The Role of Icons," 128.

34. Ibid.

35. *Homily* 10.5, quoted in ibid., 129–30.

36. Thomas F. Matthews, quoted in ibid., 130.

37. Northrop Frye, *The Great Code: The Bible and Literature* (New York: Harcourt Brace Jovanovich, 1982), 116–17.

INDEX

~ ✠ ~